Praise for Verlyn Klinkenborg's

SEVERAL SHORT SENTENCES ABOUT WRITING

"To paraphrase Voltaire's statement concerning the Almighty, 'if Verlyn Klinkenborg did not exist, it would be necessary to invent him.' Because having read *Several Short Sentences About Writing*, I do not think that it would be possible to not have this book on hand. . . . Indeed, no other book is as filled with as much grounded, practical advice for putting words to the paper or electronic page or gives better, more helpful exercises." —*New York Journal of Books*

"Klinkenborg does away with much of the traditional wisdom on writing and dissects the sentence—its structure, its intention, its semantic craftsmanship—to deliver a new, useful, and direct guide to the art of storytelling." —*Brain Pickings*

"Expertise and zeal are required for an established writer to offer genuinely useful guidance to aspiring writers. It also helps if the writer teaches writing, as Klinkenborg has for many years. . . . The result is a unique anatomy of the sentence and the writing mind and a clarifying and invigorating 'book of first steps.'" —*Booklist*

Verlyn Klinkenborg

SEVERAL SHORT SENTENCES
ABOUT WRITING

Verlyn Klinkenborg is a member of the editorial board of *The New York Times*, to which he also contributes meditations about his farm in upstate New York, collected in *The Rural Life* and *More Scenes from the Rural Life*. His other books include *Making Hay*, *The Last Fine Time*, and *Timothy; or, Notes of an Abject Reptile*. Klinkenborg has a Ph.D. in English literature from Princeton University.

Several Short Sentences About Writing

SEVERAL SHORT SENTENCES
ABOUT WRITING

Verlyn Klinkenborg

VINTAGE BOOKS
A DIVISION OF RANDOM HOUSE, INC.
NEW YORK

FIRST VINTAGE BOOKS EDITION, APRIL 2013

The Library of Congress has cataloged the Knopf edition as follows:
Klinkenborg, Verlyn.
Several short sentences about writing / Verlyn Klinkenborg. — 1st ed.
p. cm.
1. Authorship. 2. Rhetoric. I. Title.
PN151.K47 2012
808—dc23 2011050745

Vintage ISBN: 978-0-307-27941-5

Author photograph © Verlyn Klinkenborg
Book design by Soonyoung Kwon

www.vintagebooks.com

Printed in the United States of America
20

To John, Jill, and Jake

The subject is *there* only by
the grace of the author's language.

—Joyce Carol Oates

This is a book of first steps. Their meaning will change as your experience changes. This book contains the bones of many arguments and observations—a vertebra here, a mandible there—but the whole skeleton is what you make of it. You'll find as much about thought and perception here as you will about language. There are no rules, only experiments.

The premise of this book is that most of the received wisdom about how writing works is not only wrong but harmful. This is not an assumption. It's a conclusion.

Like most received wisdom, what people think they know about writing works in subtle, subterranean ways. For some reason, we seem to believe most strongly in the stuff that gets into our heads without our knowing or remembering how it got there. What we think we know about writing sounds plausible. It confirms our generally false ideas about creativity and genius. But none of this means it's true.

What I've learned about writing I've learned by trial and error, which is how most writers have learned. I had to overcome my academic training, which taught me to write in a way that was useless to me (and almost everyone else). Unlearning what I learned in college—teaching myself to write well—is the basis of what I know. So is a lifetime of reading and a love of language. The rest comes from years of writing and teaching writing. The ideas and suggestions in this book have been tested again and again, by me, by my students, and by writers who have figured these things out for themselves.

A couple of cautions before you begin. This book isn't meant to replace the received wisdom. "Received" means untested, untried, repeated out of habit. Everything in this book is meant to be tested all over again, by you. You decide what works for you. This is perhaps the most important thing I have to say. There's no gospel here, no orthodoxy, no dogma. Part of the struggle in learning to write is learning to ignore what isn't useful to you and pay attention to what is. If that means arguing with me as you read this book, so be it.

This is a book full of starting points. Perhaps they'll help you find enough clarity in your own mind and your own writing to discover what it means to write. I don't mean "write the way I do" or "write the way they do." I mean "write the way you do."

Here's a starting point. You may have no idea what way you write. I hope this book will help you find out.

Note: I use the word "piece" a lot. It means whatever you're writing, whatever the genre, whatever the length.

Several Short Sentences About Writing

Here, in short, is what I want to tell you.
Know what each sentence says,
What it doesn't say,
And what it implies.
Of these, the hardest is knowing what each sentence
actually says.

At first, it will help to make short sentences,
Short enough to feel the variations in length.
Leave space between them for the things that words
can't really say.

Pay attention to rhythm, first and last.

Imagine it this way:
One by one, each sentence takes the stage.
It says the very thing it comes into existence to say.
Then it leaves the stage.
It doesn't help the next one up or the previous one
down.
It doesn't wave to its friends in the audience
Or pause to be acknowledged or applauded.
It doesn't talk about what it's saying.
It simply says its piece and leaves the stage.

This isn't the whole art of writing well.
It isn't even most of it.
But it's a place to begin, and to begin from again and
again.

. . .

Short sentences aren't hard to make.
The difficulty is forcing yourself to keep them short.

There are innumerable ways to write badly.
The usual way is making sentences that don't say what you think they do.
Which can the reader possibly believe? Your sentences or you?

The only link between you and the reader is the sentence you're making.
There's no sign of your intention apart from the sentences themselves,
And every sentence has its own motives, its own commitments,
Quite apart from yours.
It adheres to a set of rules—grammar, syntax, the history and customs of the language, a world of echoes and allusions and social cues—that pay no heed to your intentions,
If you don't heed those rules.

It's hard to pay attention to what your words are actually saying.
As opposed to what you mean to say or what you think they're saying.
Knowing what you're trying to say is always important.
But knowing what you've actually said is crucial.
It's easier to tell what you're saying in a short sentence.

. . .

You've been taught to believe that short sentences are childish,
Merely a first step toward writing longer sentences.
You'd like to think your education has carried you well past short sentences.
But you've been delivered into a wilderness of false assumptions and bad habits,
A desert of jargon and weak constructions, a land of linguistic barbarism,
A place where it's nearly impossible to write with clarity or directness,
Without clichés or meaningless phrases.
True, you can sound quite grown-up, quite authoritative, in the manner of college professors and journalists and experts in every field.
(You may *be* a college professor, a journalist, or an expert in some field.)
How well do they write?
How much do you enjoy reading them?

You'll make long sentences again, but they'll be short sentences at heart.
Sentences listening for the silence around them.
Listening for their own pulse.

Here's an experiment:
Pay attention to all the noise in your head as you go about writing.

. . .

Much of it is what you already know about writing,
which includes:
The voices of former teachers, usually uttering rules.
Rules like, "Don't begin sentences with 'and.'"
      (It's okay. You can begin sentences with
"and.")
The things everybody knows or assumes about writers
and how they work,
Whether they're true or not.
The things you feel you must or mustn't do, without
really knowing why.
The things that make you wonder, "Am I allowed
to . . . ?"
      (Yes, you're allowed to. Not forever and
always, but until you decide for yourself what works
and what doesn't.)

Write these things down—the contents of the noise in
your head as you write.
You can't revise or discard what you don't consciously
recognize.

These assumptions and prohibitions and obligations
are the imprint of your education and the culture you
live in.
Distrust them.

What you don't know about writing is also a form of
knowledge, though much harder to grasp.
Try to discern the shape of what you don't know and

why you don't know it,
Whenever you get a glimpse of your ignorance.
Don't fear it or be embarrassed by it.
Acknowledge it.
What you don't know and why you don't know it are
information too.

Let's make a simple list from the preceding lines:

1. What you've been taught.
2. What you assume is true because you've heard it
   repeated by others.
3. What you feel, no matter how subtle.
4. What you don't know.
5. What you learn from your own experience.

These are the ways we know nearly everything about
the world around us.
Keep them in mind, especially when you begin to
think about *what* to write and *how* to write about it.

Let's think about what you already know.

In your head, you'll probably find two models for
writing.
One is the familiar model taught in high school and
college—a matter of outlines and drafts and transitions
and topic sentences and argument.

. . .

The other model is its antithesis—the way poets and novelists are often thought to write.
Words used to describe this second model include "genius," "inspiration," "flow," and "natural," sometimes even "organic."

Both models are useless.
I should qualify that sentence.
Both models are completely useless.

Loosely linked to these models are two assumptions:

  1. Many people assume there's a correlation between sentence length and the sophistication or complexity of an idea or thought—even intelligence generally.
  There isn't.

  2. Many people assume there's a correlation between the reader's experience while reading and the writer's experience while writing—her state of mind, her ease or difficulty in putting words together.
  There isn't.

You can say smart, interesting, complicated things using short sentences.
How long is a good idea?

Does it become less good if it's expressed in two sentences instead of one?

Learn to distrust words like "genius," "inspiration," "flow," "natural," and "organic" when you think about your work.

     (Don't use them when you talk about it either.)
They have nothing to do with writing
And everything to do with venerating writers.

Why short sentences?
They'll sound strange for a while until you can hear what they're capable of.
But they carry you back to a prose you can control,
To a stage in your education when your diction—your vocabulary—was under control too.
Short sentences make it easier to examine the properties of the sentence.

     (Learn to diagram sentences. It's easy.)
They help eliminate transitions.
They make ambiguity less likely and easier to detect.

There's nothing wrong with well-made, strongly constructed, purposeful long sentences.
But long sentences often tend to collapse or break down or become opaque or trip over their awkwardness.
They're pasted together with false syntax
And rely on words like "with" and "as" to lengthen the sentence.

They're short on verbs, weak in syntactic vigor,
Full of floating, unattached phrases, often out of position.
And worse—the end of the sentence commonly forgets its beginning,
As if the sentence were a long, weary road to the wrong place.

Writing short sentences restores clarity, the directness of subject and verb.
It forces you to discard the strong elements of long sentences,
Like relative pronouns and subordinate clauses,
And the weak ones as well:
Prepositional chains, passive constructions, and dependent phrases.

Writing short sentences will help you write strong, balanced sentences of any length.
Strong, lengthy sentences are really just strong, short sentences joined in various ways.

You don't have to write short sentences forever.
Only until you find a compelling reason for a long sentence
That's as clear and direct as a short sentence.
You'll be tempted to say, "But short sentences sound so choppy."
Only a string of choppy sentences sounds choppy.
Think about variation and rhythm,

The rhythm created by two or three sentences working together,
Rhythm as sound and echo but also rhythm as placement.
Learn to use the position of a sentence, the position of a word—
First? last?—as an intensifier, an accent in itself.
Can a short sentence sound like a harbinger? An adumbration?
Can it sound like a reprise or a coda?
Listen.

How short is short?
That depends on the length of the sentences you're used to writing.
One way to keep sentences short is to keep the space between them as empty as possible.
I don't mean the space between the period at the end of one sentence and the first word of the next.
I mean the space between the period and the *subject* of the next sentence.
That space often gets filled with unnecessary words.
Most sentences need no preamble—or postlude.

It's perfectly possible to make wretched short sentences.
But it's hard to go on making them for long because they sound so wretched
And because it's easy to fix them.
Making them longer is *not* the way to fix them.

. . .

To make short sentences, you need to remove every unnecessary word.
Your idea of *necessary* will change as your experience changes.
The fact that you've included a word in the sentence you're making
Says nothing about its necessity.
See which words the sentence can live without,
No matter how inconspicuous they are.
Every word is optional until it proves to be essential,
Something you can only determine by removing words one by one
And seeing what's lost or gained.
Listen for the sentence that's revealed as you remove one word after another.
You'll hear the improvement when you find it.
Try, for instance, removing the word "the."
See when the sentence can do without it and when it can't.

Without extraneous words or phrases or clauses, there will be room for implication.

The longer the sentence, the less it's able to imply,
And writing by implication should be one of your goals.
Implication is almost nonexistent in the prose that surrounds you,

The prose of law, science, business, journalism, and
most academic fields.
It was nonexistent in the way you were taught to write.
That means you don't know how to use one of a writ-
er's most important tools:
The ability to suggest more than the words seem to
allow,
The ability to speak to the reader in silence.

———————

Why are we talking about sentences?
Why not talk about the work as a whole, about shape,
form, genre, the book, the feature story, the profile,
even the paragraph?

The answer is simple.
Your job as a writer is making sentences.
Most of your time will be spent making sentences in
your head.
In your head.
Did no one ever tell you this?
That is the writer's life.
Never imagine you've left the level of the sentence
behind.

Most of the sentences you make will need to be killed.
The rest will need to be fixed.
This will be true for a long time.

The hard part now is deciding which to kill and which to fix and how to fix them.
This will get much, much easier, but the decision making will never end.

A writer's real work is the endless winnowing of sentences,
The relentless exploration of possibilities,
The effort, over and over again, to see in what you started out to say
The possibility of saying something you didn't know you could.

Shape, form, structure, genre, the whole—these have a way of clarifying themselves when sentences become clear.
Once you can actually see your thoughts and perceptions,
It's surprising how easy it is to arrange them or discover their arrangement.
This always comes as a revelation.

———————

What we're working on precedes genre.
For our purposes, genre is meaningless.
It's a method of shelving books and awarding prizes.

Every form of writing turns the world into language.
Fiction and nonfiction resemble each other far more closely than they do any actual event.

Their techniques are essentially the same, apart from sheer invention.
This is not to disparage accuracy, sound research, and impartiality.
Those are wonderful tools for novelists.

I'm interested in the genre of the sentence,
The genre that's always overlooked.
Many writers seem to believe we live in a universe of well-defined literary forms:
The memoir, the profile, the feature, the first novel, the book proposal,
A list of predetermined, prescriptive linguistic shapes
Heaped on a wagon and headed to market.

Writers worry about these shapes and their dictates
Long before they're able to make sentences worth reading.
They aspire to be nature writers,
Forgetting that nature, as a subject, is only as valid as your writing makes it.
They feel the formal burden of the memoir pressing upon them,
Though there's no such thing.
They believe that writing prose is as formulaic as writing a screenplay,
As ruled as a sonnet.
They believe the genre they've chosen
Determines the way they should write,
Complete with a road map, if only they could find it.

. . .

But genres are merely outlines by another name.
Better to be discovering what's worth discovering,
Noticing what you notice,
And putting it into sentences that, from the very beginning,
Open the reader's trust and curiosity,
Creating a willingness in the reader to see what you've discovered,
No matter what genre you call it.
Or, better yet, make the reader forget about genre completely.

If you make strong, supple sentences,
Improvise, understand and exploit your mistakes,
Keep yourself open to the possibilities each sentence creates,
Keep yourself open to thought itself,
And read like a writer,
You can write in any form.

———————————

You already possess some important assets.
You know how to talk.
How to read.
And, presumably, how to listen.
You've grown up in language.
You have the evidence of your senses.
The upwelling of your emotions.

The persistent flow of thoughts through your mind.
The habit of talking to yourself or staging conversations in your head.
Imagination and memory.
With luck, you were read aloud to as a child.
So you know how sentences sound when read aloud
And how stories are shaped and a great deal about rhythm,
Almost as much as you did when you were ten years old.
You may even have the capacity of knowing what interests you—
Or, better yet, knowing how to detect what interests you.

You're also two people, writer and reader.
This is a tremendous asset.

You can only become a better writer by becoming a better reader.
You have far more experience as a reader than you do as a writer.
You've read millions of words arranged by other writers.
How many sentences have you made so far?

But you've been taught to read in a way that tells you almost nothing about how to write
Or what's really to be found in the books you read.

.   .   .

You were taught that reading is extraction.

You learned to gather something called meaning from
what you read,
As if the words themselves were merely smoke signals
Blowing away in the breeze, leaving a trace of cognition in the brain.
You've been taught, too, that writing is the business of
depositing *meaning* to be extracted later,
That a sentence is the transcription of a thought, the
husk of an idea,
Valuable only for what it transmits or contains, not for
what it is.
You've been taught to overlook the character of the
prose in front of you in order to get at its *meaning*.
You overlook the shape of the sentence itself for the
meaning it contains,
Which means that while you were reading,
All those millions of words passed by
Without teaching you how to make sentences.

We take for granted, as a premise barely worth examining, that changing the words in a sentence—even the
order of words—must have an effect on its meaning.
And yet we think and read and write as if the fit
between language and meaning were approximate,
As though many different sentences were capable of
meaning the same thing.

·   ·   ·

Our conventional idea of meaning is something like,
"what can be restated."
It means a summary.
It means "in other words."

You know how to theorize and summarize,
How to identify ideologies in the texts you read.
You do very well on the reading comprehension por-
tion of the test.
But no one said a word about following a trail of com-
mon sense
Through the underbrush of the sentences themselves.
No one showed you the affinities at work among those
thickets of ink
Or explained that the whole life of the language
Lies in the solidity of the sentence and cannot be extracted.

Writing well and reading well mean paying attention
to *all* the subtleties embodied in a sentence
In its exact form and no other.

How many subtleties?
What kinds?
That depends on how perceptive you become.

No two sentences are the same unless they're exactly
the same, word for word.

(And, in a lifetime of writing, it's unlikely
you'll ever write the same sentence twice.)

Any variation in wording changes the nuances that emanate from the sentence.

Discovering those nuances, and using them, are parts of the writer's job.

We'll discover a few shortly.

———————————

But first, what if *meaning* isn't the sole purpose of the sentence?

What if it's only the chief attribute among many, a tool, among others, that helps the writer shape or revise the sentence?

What if the virtue, the value, of the sentence is the sentence itself and not its extractable meaning?

What if you wrote as though sentences can't be summarized?

What if you value every one of a sentence's attributes and not merely its *meaning*?

Strangely enough, this is how you read when you were a child.

Children read repetitively and with incredible exactitude.

They demand the very sentence—word for word—and no other.

The *meaning* of the sentence is never a substitute for the sentence itself,

Not to a six-year-old.

.   .   .

This is still an excellent way to read.

The purpose of a sentence is to say what it has to say
but also to be itself,
Not merely a substrate for the extraction of *meaning*.

The words in a sentence have a degree of specificity or
concreteness.
They have complex histories.
They derive from dense contexts—literature, culture,
the worlds of work.
They've been shaped by centuries of writing,
Centuries of utterance by living human beings.
They resonate with the ghosts of all their earlier forms.

The sentence itself has a rhythm.
It has velocity.
It uses metaphor and simile
Or hyperbole or metonymy or alliteration or internal
rhyme or one of hundreds of other rhetorical devices.
It helps define the dramatic gesture that you—the
writer—are making in the piece.
It stirs or gratifies the reader's expectations, on many
levels.
It identifies the reader.
It gives the reader pause.
It names the world, using the actual names the world
already contains.
Perhaps it renames the world.
And this is only the beginning.

You're the curator of all these qualities in the sentences
you make,
Which lie there almost unnoticed
If you're interested only in extracting or depositing
meaning.

Your task isn't merely to write with these qualities in
mind.
It's to read with them in mind too,
You're learning to write, gathering materials to write
From everything you read as well as everything you
write
And from everything you notice in the world around
you.
Learning to write begins anywhere, at any time in life.

———————

There's another trouble with *meaning*.
We've been taught to believe it comes near the end.
As if the job of all those sentences were to ferry us
along to the place where meaning is enacted—to "the
point,"
Just before the conclusion,
Which restates "the point."

This is especially true in the school model of writing.
Remember the papers you wrote?
Trying to save that one good idea till the very end?
Hoping to create the illusion that it followed logically

from the previous paragraphs?
You were stalling until you had ten pages.

Much of what's taught under the name of expository
writing could be called "The Anxiety of Sequence."
Its premise is this:
To get where you're going, you have to begin in just
the right place
And take the proper path,
Which depends on knowing where you plan to conclude.

This is like not knowing where to begin a journey
Until you decide where you want it to end.
Begin in the wrong place, make the wrong turn,
And there's no getting where you want to go.

Why not begin where you already are?
Is there only the one way to get where you're going?

You were taught in school that each sentence
Rests on all the others like a single card in a house of
cards,
A carefully constructed house of logic,
Fragile and easily dislodged.

That's one reason school papers often begin with sev-
eral false starts.
The piece proceeds after the third introductory paragraph
And usually has two conclusions.

. . .

You were taught so much about outlining and transitions and the appearance of logic.

Perhaps you face the difficulties you do
Because you were taught so much about outlining
And transitions and the appearance of logic.

You were given a model of writing in which the sentences,
Inextricably overlapping, seamlessly transitioning,
Point forward toward the conclusion that justifies their existence.

———————

In school you learned to write as if the reader
Were in constant danger of getting lost,
A problem you were taught to solve not by writing clearly
But by shackling your sentences and paragraphs together.

Think about transitions.
Remember how it goes?
Late in the paragraph you prepare for the transition to the next paragraph—
The great leap over the void, across that yawning indentation.
You were taught the art of the flying trapeze,
But not how to write.

. . .

Why were you taught to dwell on transitions?
It was assumed that you can't write clearly
And that even if you could write clearly,
The reader needs a handrail through your prose.
What does that say about the reader?
That the reader is essentially passive and in need of constant herding.

Are *you* that kind of reader?
Do you tumble, uncomprehending, through the gaps between paragraphs?
Do you trip over ellipses?
Do you require constant supervision while walking down corridors of prose?
Do you lose the writer's train of thought unless you're reminded of it constantly?

No sentence can afford to be merely transitional.
If you've written clearly—
And you know what you've said and implied
As surely as you know what you haven't said—
The reader will never get lost reading your prose
Or have trouble following you *without* transitions.
A reader is likelier to get lost cutting his way through
The jungle of transitions than crossing the gap of a well-made ellipsis.

And what about topic sentences?
Their only purpose is to announce the subject of the paragraph you're about to read,

As if you'd never figure it out otherwise.
In journalism, the equivalent of the topic sentence is
the notorious "nut graf,"
A paragraph that tells you the content of the article
you're about to read,
As if you couldn't proceed without a précis.

The obsession with transition negates a basic truth
about writing,
A magical truth.
You can get anywhere from anywhere,
Always and almost instantly.
The gap between sentences is sometimes a pause for
breath
And sometimes an echoing void.
And if you can get anywhere from anywhere,
You can start anywhere
And end anywhere.
There is no single necessary order.

Here's another basic truth.
Prose isn't validated by a terminal *meaning*.
If you love to read—as surely you must—you love
being wherever you find yourself in the book you're
reading,
Happy to be in the presence of every sentence as it
passes by,
Not biding your time until the *meaning* comes along.

· · ·

Writing isn't a conveyer belt bearing the reader to "the point" at the end of the piece, where the *meaning* will be revealed.
Good writing is significant everywhere,
Delightful everywhere.

The transitions you use should exist for the love of transition,
To employ and honor our abiding affection
For the *turn* that so often takes place in our reading,
The *turn* when the story changes or redirects itself.
They recall the moment, as children, when we came upon the phrase
"And then one day."

You know exactly how those four words feel.
You know exactly what they do.
When you get lost in your writing, remember them.
Don't use them: think about the possibilities they contain.
The ability to gather and redirect,
To rise above the level of the prose and look around,
As if you were standing in a crow's nest
Looking out over a sea of words,
Detecting a shift in the wind,
A change in the current,
A new impetus in your expectations,
And pointing it out to the reader.

. . .

That's a transition.
You knew how it worked and felt
When you were barely old enough to read.

The transitions you were taught in school are merely
The nervous stitching together of sentences and paragraphs,
A cross-hatching of self-reference.

The syntactic result of all that connecting and tran-
sitioning—
Linking sentences and paragraphs to each other—
Is the very stuff you cut away in order to write
Short sentences
And make yourself intelligible again.

The extra space you feel between short sentences is mostly
The missing apparatus of transition and connection.

———————

The anxiety about transition isn't caused only by
The prospect of a reader losing her way between paragraphs.

It's also caused by the period at the end of a sentence,
As if the period marks a boundary of comprehension.
This is one of the ways long sentences happen.

. . .

Most overcrowded sentences can be broken apart easily.
They became overcrowded because the words and
phrases and thoughts they contain
Somehow seemed to belong together
In the shelter found to the left of the period,
The writer huddling words and phrases together into a
single long sentence.

Related ideas coexisting side by side in two or three
short sentences
Doesn't seem to be good enough:
They must live together in the same ramshackle
sentence.

A crowded sentence betrays the writer's worry that the
reader won't follow the prose
If parted by a period.
It also betrays the writer's lassitude,
The lazy shuffling of words together into a single
sentence
Instead of deciding what really matters
And finding the verbal energy to construct separate
sentences.

A single crowded sentence means giving up all the
possible relations
Among shorter sentences—the friction, the tension,
The static electricity that builds up between them.
A single crowded sentence has only itself to relate to,
Only an enervated communion among its parts.

What else were you learning?
You were learning to dodge the "I" in your prose—
And yet to sound coy when indulging in it,
As though you were writing in front of a mirror.

In writing nonfiction, were you ever asked to *be* the narrator,
To speak directly to the reader,
To decide what dramatic gesture you were making and act upon it?
Were you asked to write in order to be heard, to be listened to?
Asked to write a piece that mattered to you?
Was there ever a satisfactory answer to the question,
"Why am I telling you this?"
Besides "It's due on Monday"?

You were taught the perfect insincerity of the writing exercise,
Asked to write pieces in which you didn't and couldn't believe.
You learned a strange ventriloquism,
Saying things you were implicitly being asked to say,
Knowing that no one was really listening.
You were being taught to write as part of a transaction that had
Almost nothing to do with real communication,
Learning to treat the making of sentences as busywork,

A groping for words, an act of drudgery,
A way of dressing up your meaning or your argument
with almost no attention to the character of the words
or sentences you were using,
Unless you were trying to imitate
The stiff and impersonal manner of "formal" prose.

You were also learning to distrust the reader and yourself.

Do you remember feeling, when you were writing a
paper for school,
That your vocabulary was steadily shrinking?
By the end, the same few words seemed to be buzzing
Around and around in your head, like flies weary of
feeding.
That's a symptom of boredom.
You were bored from the start and for good reason.
You were repeatedly asked to persuade or demonstrate
or argue,
To reiterate or prove or recite or exemplify,
To go through the motions of writing.
You were almost never asked to notice or observe, wit-
ness or testify.
You were being taught to manage the evidence gath-
ered from other authorities
Instead of cultivating your own—
To simulate logic
But not to write so clearly that
What you were saying seemed self-evident.

.   .   .

You were also learning to divorce your experience as
a reader
From your inexperience as a writer.
When what you needed most was to trust your experience as a reader.

––––––––––––

In school, we're taught—or we absorb the idea—that
writing
Flows out of the creative writer like lava down the
slope of a volcano.
An uninterruptible stream.
And yet we study the work itself as if its molten fire
had hardened into rock.

But the work isn't an eruption from the author's brain.
It doesn't merely flow.
And it remains more dynamic, as written—on the
page—than we let ourselves imagine.

We forget something fundamental as we read:
Every sentence could have been otherwise but isn't.
We can't see all the decisions that led to the final shape
of the sentence.
But we can see the residue of those decisions.

If you look at the manuscripts of writers—
Handwritten drafts preserved in museums and
libraries—

You can often see the changes they made scribbled between the lines.
What you can't see are the changes they made in their heads before those sentences were ever inscribed.

If you could look through the spaces between the sentences,
Through the door into the writing room, into that writer's head,
You'd see that every word was different once
And that the writer was contemplating
An incalculable number of differences,
Feeling her way among the alternatives that presented themselves,
Until settling upon words that were finally written down,
Then revised over and over again—
Before they were printed, published, reprinted in anthologies,
And treated as though they'd been carved in stone.

It was all change until the very last second.

Every work of literature is the result of thousands and thousands of decisions.
Intricate, minute decisions—this word or that, here or where, now or later, again and again.
It's the living tissue of a writer's choices,
Not the fossil record of an ancient, inspired race.
Interrogate those choices.

Imagine the reason behind each sentence.
Why is it shaped just this way and not some other way?
Why that choice of words?
Why that phrasing?
Why that rhythm?

The purpose of these questions isn't to construct a theory,
A hypothesis about how or why the writer writes.
The purpose is to help you notice the shape of what lies before you.
The answers to these questions may be nothing more than
Noticing the effect of asking them.

Imagine reading Jane Austen or James Baldwin and wondering,
Why is the sentence this way and not another way?
That sounds like a trivial or unanswerable question.
Until you imagine revising the sentence, giving it a different rhythm,
Substituting a different word, a different structure.
Revise a sentence by Austen or Baldwin?
Why not? It's an experiment.
Try it, and you begin to glimpse the inherent necessity binding the writer's choices together.
You begin to see the invisible tensions that arc from line to line,
Paragraph to paragraph, page to page.

These aren't constructions of logic or meaning.
They're echoes and responses, moments of candor and
their aftereffects,
Feats of resilience and attention, sound and impulsion.

"Why is this sentence this way?"
Finds its answer in
"Why is that sentence that way?"
Which sounds circular, until you begin to understand
how
Each variation shapes and affirms others,
Creating the restraint of good prose,
A balance of forces and internal tensions
That make the minutest effects discernible.

This isn't a description of the writer's genius or inspira-
tion or intention.
It describes the way every sentence influences every
other sentence.
It describes the writer's alertness to her sentences.
The way her sentences listen to one another.

Prose is the residue, the consequence, of the writer's
choices,
Choices about the shape of each sentence
And how each sentence shapes the others.

That's how we need to read, as writers—
Paying attention to the decisions embedded in each
sentence,

Decisions visible in the structure of the sentence itself.
What you write—what you send out into the world
to be read—
Is the residue of the choices and decisions *you* make.
Choices and decisions *you* are responsible for.

And what are the choices?
That's like asking, what are the nuances?
It depends on how perceptive you become.

––––––––––––

The central fact of your education is this:
You've been taught to believe that what you discover
by thinking,
By examining your own thoughts and perceptions,
Is unimportant and unauthorized.
As a result, you fear thinking,
And you don't believe your thoughts are interesting,
Because you haven't learned to be interested in them.

There's another possibility:
You may be interested in your thoughts,
But they don't have much to do with anything you've
ever been asked to write.

The same is true of what you notice.
You don't even notice what you notice,
Because nothing in your education has taught you that
what you notice is important.

And if you do notice something that interests you,
It doesn't have much to do with anything you've ever
been asked to write.

But everything you notice is important.
Let me say that a different way:
If you notice something, it's because it's important.
But what you notice depends on what you allow your-
self to notice,
And that depends on what you feel authorized, per-
mitted to notice
In a world where we're trained to disregard our perceptions.

Who's going to give you the authority to feel that what
you notice is important?
It will have to be you.
The authority you feel has a great deal to do with how
you write, and what you write,
With your ability to pay attention to the shape and
meaning of your own thoughts
And the value of your own perceptions.

Being a writer is an act of perpetual self-authorization.
No matter who you are.
Only you can authorize yourself.
You do that by writing well, by constant discovery.
No one else can authorize you.
No one.
This doesn't happen overnight.
It's as gradual as the improvement in your writing.

. . .

Start by learning to recognize what interests you.
Most people have been taught that what they notice
doesn't matter,
So they never learn how to notice,
Not even what interests them.
Or they assume that the world has been completely
pre-noticed,
Already sifted and sorted and categorized
By everyone else, by people with real authority.
And so they write about pre-authorized subjects in
pre-authorized language.

Why do I say this?
When students are free to write anything they want,
What they write first are pieces they hope look like
something they saw published somewhere
About subjects they believe are pre-authorized
Because someone has already written about them
In pieces they hoped looked like something they saw
published somewhere.
A first piece of that kind is a tacit way of taking shelter
under the authority of someone else's perceptions.
It's also a way of saying, "I know you're not really
interested in what I think or notice."
But that's the very thing the reader *is* interested in
If your sentences allow him to be.

Is it possible to practice noticing?
I think so.
But I also think it requires a suspension of yearning
And a pause in the desire to be pouring something out
of yourself.
Noticing is about letting yourself out into the world,
Rather than siphoning the world into you
In order to transmute it into words.

Practicing noticing will also help you learn more about
patience
And the nature of your mind.
Noticing means thinking with all your senses.
It's also an exercise in not writing.

So what is noticing?
A pinpoint of awareness,
The detail that stands out amid all the details.
It's catching your sleeve on the thorn of the thing you
notice
And paying attention as you free yourself.

It requires no gear, no special tools, no apparatus.
You practice noticing as part of your ordinary life.

What do you notice? Whatever you notice.
Behavior, thought, overheard words, light, resemblance,
Emotion, totality, particularity,
Whatever you find in the habitat of your perceptions,

Anything, no matter how minute,
Whether you're working or reading or taking the
subway.
The pattern is particular to you,
An element in what gets construed as "style."

What you notice has no meaning.
Be sure to assign it none.
It doesn't represent or symbolize
Or belong to some world theory or allegory of perception.
Don't put words to it.
And don't collect it. Let it slip away.
Be patient for the next thing you notice.

There's always an urge among writers
To turn fleeting observations and momentary glimpses
Into metaphors and "material" as quickly as possible,
As if every perception ended in a trope,
As if the writer were a dynamo
Turning the world into words.
The goal is the opposite:
To get your words, your phrases,
As close as you can to the solidity,
The materiality of the world you're noticing.

Rushing to notice never works,
Nor does trying to notice.
Attention requires a cunning passivity.

. . .

Let yourself wonder why this thing, this instant, this suddenness, caught your attention.
What you're noticing isn't only what struck you.
It's also how your mind, your attention, gets from place to place,
From the steady current of your thoughts to their sudden interruption.

Notice what you notice and let it go.

You can also make sentences the way you go about practicing noticing.
Catching a phrase in your head,
Exploring the possibilities it occasions,
Then releasing it,
Making nothing more than a vanishing sentence,
Which you do not transfix in some collection of sentences
Or etherize in a jar.

You'll never run out of noticings,
And there are more than enough sentences to let a few go.

The urge to write is so strong.
Aspiring writers want so badly to be pouring something out of themselves.
You need a place where you can practice noticing and making sentences—

Observations of genuine clarity,
Sentences of vigor, invention, and self-perception.
That place would be your mind.

What you get in return for this gathering and releasing
Is habit, ease, trust, and a sense of abundance that sustains your writing.
And your mind never relinquishes what really matters.

———————————

As you practice noticing, notice how thickly particled
With names the world around you is.
This will gradually become part of your noticing,
Looking not for words to make us see the way you saw—
But for the names of what you've noticed,
Names that announce the whatness of the world
To a single species.

It's hard to grasp at first the density, the specificity
With which the world has been named.
This is a planet of overlapping lexicons,
Generation after generation, trade after trade,
Expedition after expedition sent out to bring home
Name upon name, terms of identity in endless degrees
of intricacy,
And all at hand, if you look for them.

.   .   .

Don't neglect such a rich linguistic inheritance.
It's your business to know the names of things,
To recover them if necessary and use them.
This isn't merely a matter of expanding your vocabulary.
It's a matter of understanding that everything you see and know
About your presence in this moment of perception
Is overlaid by a parallel habitat of language,
Names that lie tacit until you summon them.

And yet you've been taught to make sentences
In which inert verbs act abstractly upon faceless nouns,
To write on a theoretical basis, which deprives the world of its content,
And to use passive constructions, which absolve everyone of responsibility.

What's a metaphor in the prose you were taught to write?
A stage prop, a paraphrase, a clarification, at best,
Nearly always cumbersome, bordering on cliché,
Almost always timid, rarely serious, usually self-conscious,
And too often stretched out over three or four sentences
In order to create an extended metaphor,
Which is a cruel analogical death.

A true metaphor is a swift and violent twisting of language,

A renaming of the already named.
It's meant to expire in a sudden flash of light
And to reveal—in that burst of illumination—
A correspondence that must be literally accurate.
Any give in the metaphor, any indeterminacy,
And it becomes a cloud of smoke, not a flash of light.
Like any rhetorical device, the less you use it, the more effective it is.

Try making prose with a poetic seriousness about its tools—
Rhythm, twists of language, the capacity to show the reader
What lies beyond expression,
But with the gaits of prose and a plainness in reserve
That poetry rarely possesses, an exalted plainness.

———————

One of the hardest things about learning to read well is learning to believe that every sentence has been consciously, purposely shaped by the writer.
This is only credible in the presence of excellent writing.

You may notice, as you write, that sentences often volunteer a shape of their own
And supply their own words as if they anticipated your thinking.
Those sentences are nearly always unacceptable,

Dull and unvarying, yielding only a small number of possible structures
And only the most predictable phrases, the inevitable clichés.

A cliché is dead matter.
It causes gangrene in the prose around it, and sooner or later it eats your brain.
You can't fix a cliché by using it ironically.
You can't make it less gangrenous by appearing to "quote" it or invert it or joke about it.
A cliché isn't just a familiar, overused saying.
It's the debris of someone else's thinking,
Any group of words that seem to cluster together "naturally"
And enlist in your sentence.
The only thing to do with a cliché is send it to the sports page
Or the speechwriters, where it will live forever.

Volunteer sentences occur because you're not considering the actual sentence you're making.
You're looking past it toward your meaning somewhere down the road,
Or toward the intent of the whole piece.
Somehow that seems more important than the sentence you're actually making,
Though your meaning and the intent of the whole piece
Depend entirely on the sentence you're making.

In fact, you're distracted from the sentence by your
intention
And by wondering how soon you'll be done.
You're distracted from the only thing of any value to
the reader.

Volunteer sentences are the relics of your education
And the desire to emulate the grown-up, workaday
prose that surrounds you,
Which is made overwhelmingly of sentences that are
banal and structurally thoughtless.

A volunteer sentence is almost always a perfunctory
sentence.
That can change.
But only after years of questioning the shapes of sen-
tences you read,
And every sentence you write.
Don't let the word "years" alarm you.
Think of it as months and months and months and
months.

You may think a volunteer sentence is an inspired one
Simply because it volunteers.

This is one reason to abandon the idea of inspiration.
All the idea of inspiration will do
Is stop you from revising a volunteer sentence.
Only revision will tell you whether a sentence that
offers itself is worth keeping.

. . .

The writer's job isn't accepting sentences.
The job is making them, word by word.

Volunteer sentences,
Volunteer subjects,
Volunteer structures.
Avoid them all.

Most aspiring writers write too soon.
They think writing is a transitive act instead of an intransitive one.
Everything they know about writing—all those images of writers writing—
Hastens them to the desk,
Where they sit perched over the keyboard or pen in hand,
Caught in an anticipatory gesture,
Eyes intent on the possibilities of the screen,
Poised at the brink of thought, but not actually thinking,
As though by leaning forward a sentence will tip out of their heads
And onto the page.

But writing isn't performed upon a device or in a state of anticipation.

. . .

Consider the bad habit of typing, preliminarily, two or three words—
A natural start to the sentence, you think—
And then waiting for the rest of the sentence to reveal itself.
But after two or three words the sentence is already foredoomed,
Its structure predetermined.
Two or three words, and you've already reduced the remaining choices
To a small, depressing handful.
It's shocking to realize how quickly you become wedded to those two or three words,
How hard it is to abandon them for an alternative.

Sometimes, going over your work, you discover
That you can't remember how every sentence came to take its shape.
You come across vestiges of unconsciousness in your prose,
Amnesiac stretches where sentences seem to have written themselves.
This is not a good thing.

When the work is really complete, the writer knows how each sentence got that way,
What choices were made.
You become not only a living concordance of your work, able to say where almost any word appears.

You also carry within you the memory of all the decisions you made while shaping your prose,
Decisions invisible to the reader except in the residue
of your prose.

It sounds impossible to know so much about what
you've written.
And yet it's inevitable.
Something you don't even have to think about
If you've been thinking about your sentences.

This brings us back to the difficulty of knowing what
your sentences actually say.
The problem most writers face isn't writing.
It's consciousness.
Attention.
Noticing.
That includes noticing language.

The fundamental act of revision is literally becoming
conscious of the sentence,
Seeing it for what it is, word for word, as a shape, and
in relation to all the other sentences in the piece.

This is surprisingly hard to do at first
Because our reading habits are impatient and extractive.

And because we've been blinded to the actuality of
prose—
Its physical substance—
By the pursuit of *meaning*.

The very nature of reading encourages us to believe
we're looking *through* the prose to worlds on the other
side of the ink.

The familiarity with which we know our own lives is
sometimes disabling.
Writing is a special instance of that.
In responding to your own prose, you're responding in
some sense to yourself,
And no matter how hard you look, you're almost invis-
ible to yourself,
Camouflaged by familiarity.
One basic strategy for revision is becoming a stranger
to what you've written.

Try reading your work aloud.
The ear is much smarter than the eye,
If only because it's also slower
And because the eye can't see rhythm or hear unwanted
repetition.

But how should you read aloud?
There's self-awareness even in this,
A tendency to overdramatize or become self-conscious,

To read as though the words weren't yours,
Mechanically, without listening,
As though you were somehow hiding from their sound
Or merely fulfilling a rote obligation.

Try reading the words on the page as though they were
meant to be spoken plainly
To a listener who is both you and not you—
An imaginary listener seated not too far away.
That way your attention isn't only on the words you're
reading.
It's on the transmission of those words.
As you read aloud, catch the rhythm of the sentences
without overemphasizing it.
Read so the listener can hear the shape of the syntax.
You be the listener, not another person.
You'll be stopping often.

Reading aloud forces you to choose *how* you'll read
aloud,
What character you'll play, what version of yourself
you'll present,
What dramatic gesture you're making as you read.
The act of writing requires exactly the same thing,
Though we pretend it doesn't—
Another good reason to read your work aloud.

If you don't know what I mean by rhythm,
Imagine a singer's phrasing of the lyric in a song.

In prose, it's subtler, the beat and the music quieter.
Try reading aloud some of everything you read, no matter what it is,
A couple of paragraphs from the newspaper or a text-book or a novel or a poem.
Especially a poem.
This is how you begin to understand rhythm and its absence.

It will also improve your ability to read aloud,
Which will help you discern the underlying textures of your prose.
How well you read aloud reveals how well you understand the syntax of a sentence.
Do you remember, in school, going around the room,
Each student in turn reading a paragraph out loud?
Remember how well some students read and others, how badly?
It was a difference in comprehension,
Not of the sentence's *meaning,*
But of its texture, pace, structure, actuality.

———————

Don't read straight through without stopping.
Read until your ear detects a problem.
Stop there.
How will you know there's a problem?
Something will sound funny.

You'll feel a subtle disturbance, a nameless, barely discernible tremor inside you.
You won't say, "Aha! That pronoun has the wrong
antecedent!"
      (Though soon you will.)
You'll simply feel that something's wrong, without
knowing what.
      (This also happens when you're reading silently,
but less emphatically.)

Pay attention now:
No matter how much you know or learn about syntax,
grammar, and rhetoric,
This small internal quaver, this inner disturbance,
Is the most useful evidence you'll ever get.
Someday, you'll be able to articulate what causes it.
But for now, what's important is to notice it.
Noticing is always the goal.
Actually, the goal right now is noticing that you're
noticing.
One day merely noticing will be enough.

You already experience these faint stirrings in the pres-
ence of sentences,
But you didn't know they mattered.
This turns out to be true of many things you notice.

No one taught you to disregard these inner sensations.
No one taught you to be aware of them either.

No one even acknowledged that they exist.
You thought they weren't significant—
Mainly because they were occurring within *you*.
And what do *you* know (you're always tempted to ask)?
You know a lot, especially in a preconscious kind of way.

Notice those stirrings now, and keep noticing.
Never stop.
They're a sign of your skill and experience as a reader,
And they're immensely useful to you as a writer always.

Writing requires a high degree of inner alertness,
Especially when things are going wrong.

Soon you'll know exactly how to find the things that are going wrong
As well as the things that are going right.
But until then—and even long after—you'll find it easier to detect a problem by the disturbance it causes inside you.

This means paying attention not only to your writing but to your emotions.
I don't mean large-scale emotions—sad, mournful, depressed, suicidal, elated.
I mean a pale and nameless unease,
As if a poorly constructed sentence could make you slightly homesick.

The faint vertigo caused by an ambiguity you can't
quite detect.
The malaise given off by an awkwardness in the syntax.
You won't be able to name the feeling a syntactical
problem causes.
It doesn't have a name.
What matters is what it points to.
Find out what's causing it and fix it
Even if you're not sure how.

———————————

Here's another way to make your prose look less
familiar.
Turn every sentence into its own paragraph.
        (Hit Return after every period. If writing by
hand, begin each new sentence at the left margin.)
What happens?
A sudden, graphic display of the length of your
sentences
And, better yet, their relative length—how it varies, or
doesn't vary, from one to the next.
Variation is the life of prose, in length and in structure.

Having all your sentences in a column, one above the
other, makes them easier to examine.
Suddenly you see similarities in shape.
You notice, for instance, how your sentences cling to
each other
Instead of accepting their separateness.

And you can begin to ask questions—simple ones—
that will help you understand how to revise
And make better sentences.

How many sentences begin with the subject?
How many begin with an opening phrase *before* the
subject?
Or with a word like "When" or "Since" or "While" or
"Because"?
How many begin with "There" or "It"?
What kinds of nouns do you see?
Abstractions? Generalizations?
Multisyllabic Latinate nouns ending in "-ion"?
Or are they the solid names of actual things?
Is the subject of the sentence an actor capable of per-
forming the action of the verb?
Can you adjust the sentence so it is?
Or does the subject of the sentence hide the action of
entities that are able to act—humans, for instance?
How close is the subject to its verb?
Are they separated by an inserted phrase?
What does that do to the velocity of the sentence?
How many of the verbs are variants of "to be"—"is,"
"are," "were," "was," and so on?
Are the verbs active, energetic?
Or do they merely connect or arrange or present or
relate?
Are the constructions passive?
How often does the word "as" appear, and in which of
its many senses?

Are you using "with" as a preposition or as a false conjunction, a false relative pronoun?

Are there inadvertent repetitions—words repeated unintentionally?

Is every phrase in its proper place, every word?

Is everything next to what it should be next to?

Anything outright ungrammatical?

Words used improperly?

Do verbs that require direct objects (transitive verbs) lack them?

If there's a modifying phrase at the start of the sentence, does it modify the subject of the sentence? (It must.)

Can the sentence be broken in two or three?

Do these questions sound overly technical to you?
They're basic.
But they raise another mistaken assumption about writing.

Many people assume there's an inherent conflict between creativity and a critical, analytic awareness of the medium you work in.

They assume that the creative artist works unconsciously
And that knowing too much about matters like grammar and syntax diminishes or blunts creativity.

This is nonsense.
You don't need to be an expert in grammar and syntax to write well.

But you do need to know the difference between transitive and intransitive verbs.
Between active and passive constructions.
The relation between a pronoun and its antecedent.
All the parts of speech.
The different verb tenses.
The nature of participles and their role as modifiers.
The subtleties of prepositions—the hardest part of speech even for native speakers of English.
You need a toolbox of rhetorical devices, like irony, hyperbole,
And the various kinds of analogy.
You need an ever-growing vocabulary—and with it the awareness that most words carry several meanings.
You need to look up even familiar words every time you have a doubt
And especially when you don't have a doubt.
That is, very often.
That is, every time you write.

The history of a word is part of its meaning,
Sometimes even the better part of its meaning.
You're responsible for the nuances of the words you use.
How else can you use exactly the right shade of meaning?
How else can the reader trust you?
You can't disclaim this responsibility.
Those nuances are embedded in etymology.

.   .   .

A good example: the word *autopsia,*
Which I came across while working on a book of my
own.
I thought—by inference from the context and by anal-
ogy with "autopsy"—
That *autopsia* meant a collection of stuffed or dissected
animals,
The sort of collection a natural historian might
accumulate.
But if I had thought more carefully and considered the
word's roots,
I would have realized that it means
A collection of objects one has "seen for oneself."
I discovered that when I looked up the familiar word
"autopsy,"
Which means, etymologically, to see for oneself.
You'll need to look up nearly every word you use for
longer than you think.
It's the only way to be sure of meaning
And etymology
And pronunciation, which has a bearing on rhythm.

Think of your vocabulary as your *autopsia*—
Words you've actually seen for yourself.

———————

If you don't know the language of grammar and syntax, try this.
Begin with the parts of speech.

Copy or print out a couple of pages by an author whose work you like.

    (For example, the opening of John McPhee's *Coming into the Country*.)

Gather some colored pens or pencils.

Choose one color and circle all the nouns.

Pause to consider them.

Then choose a different color and circle all the verbs.

Pause again.

Ditto the articles, adverbs, adjectives, prepositions, conjunctions, and interjections.

Anything left over?

There shouldn't be.

This will clarify the parts of speech, and it will help you see how the author uses them.

If a word puzzles you, look it up.

A good dictionary will tell you what part of speech it is.

Don't just imagine doing this someday.

Do it. It's interesting.

Now try a slightly harder version of this experiment on a separate copy.

Circle the direct objects.

The indirect objects.

The participles.

The relative pronouns.

The metaphors and similes and analogies.

Any word that seems to be used in a way that distorts its meaning.

Any particularly rhythmic phrases or sentences.
Any spot where you sense a change in direction or time
or voice.
Any phrase that interests you.
Any word that stops you.
Anything you *notice*, whether you think it matters or
not.
It matters because you noticed it.

Do any of the words surprise you or call attention to
themselves?
I'm not asking whether you know what they mean.
You've already looked up every word you don't know.
Haven't you?

It's easier to answer a comparative question
Than a question that depends on an implicit standard
of judgment.
"Is this sentence longer than that one?" is easier to
answer than
"Is that word poetic?"
You don't need much experience to tell whether one
sentence is longer than another.
But you do to say whether a word is poetic in usage.
That experience is easy to come by.
It's called "reading poetry."
Turn to the poets.
Learn from them.

. . .

At first, ask comparative questions.
They'll help you understand how writing works.
Examine the quantities that appear in prose—
The things that can be measured or counted:
Rhythms, patterns of repetition, length of words and
sentences,
Length of paragraphs, the breadth of an ellipsis.
Examine the distance between sentences.
Some lie close together, making small steps forward.
Others seem to stand well apart from each other,
Advancing the piece discontinuously.

These kinds of questions will help you understand
The character of what you're reading and how it was
made.
We take for granted that what we love in our reading is
Perception, wisdom, poetry, wit, irony.
Yet it's surprising how often what we love is really
found in the material structure, the concrete details,
the rhythm of the sentences.

Ask yourself questions about the words you find—
especially less ordinary or less familiar words.
            (But query the familiar ones too.)
Where do they come from?
What line of work are they in?
Who's likely to use them?
And in what context?
This will remind you that every word carries a social
freight.

Now perform the same experiment with an author whose work has a different feel.

(Try Joan Didion's essay "Some Dreamers of the Golden Dream" in *Slouching Towards Bethlehem*.)

Then try it again with a page from a very different context—
A business article or a best seller or a critical essay in an academic journal.

What do you find?
Different patterns of usage, different lexicons,
Which create, in turn, different textures and rhythms in the sentences themselves.

Try the same experiment on some pages of your own prose.
What do you notice?

Make some comparative lists:
How does the menagerie of Didion's nouns compare with the menagerie of McPhee's nouns or the nouns in a critical essay or a business article—or something you're writing?
Ask the same question about verbs and sentence structures.
Ask yourself too how present the writer feels to the reader.

How strong is your sense of the speaker or narrator?
How is that sense created, and where do you detect it?

Imagine it this way:
Every piece is an ecosystem of words and structures
and rhythms.
How rich and diverse is the ecosystem in each of these
pieces?
From which do you derive the most pleasure?
And why?

Be patient with yourself and the things you discover.
This isn't a test.
Every reader will notice different things.
You won't know the significance of everything you
notice.
Don't let that deter you.
Don't try to give a *meaning* to the things you notice.
Just observe them.
Again, the effect of these discoveries may be nothing
more than
Noticing the effect of making these discoveries.
You'll become much more adept at seeing how your
own sentences are shaped and where they succeed and
go awry.

Thinking in terms of grammar and syntax is also a
good way to make your sentences seem less familiar.

Suddenly you're looking at their bones and muscles,
The way they're joined and the kinetics of their movement.

But notice.
The point of learning the fundamental language of grammar and syntax
Isn't correctness or obeying the rules.
It's keeping the rules from obtruding themselves upon the reader
Because you've ignored them.

The reader is just like you,
Full of subtle, distracting feelings when things are going wrong in a sentence.

Every reader is always two readers.
One reads with a deep, intuitive feel for the way language works
And yet with overwhelming literalness.
This reader (no matter what he consciously knows about grammar or syntax) is troubled by mistakes, misspellings,
And especially the syntactical miscues that cause ambiguity.
This reader will always stumble over your errors.
If a sentence offers an ambiguous path—two ways of being read—this reader will always take the wrong one.

.   .   .

The other reader—literate, curious, adaptable, intelligent, open-minded—
Will follow you anywhere you want to go
As long as your prose is clear.
       (More on this excellent person soon.)
Every reader is both of these readers in one.
Write for both together.

Here's another reason for learning the basics of grammar and syntax:
Syntactic and grammatical accuracy is the precondition for being sure
Your sentences say what you think they say.

It's no trouble to learn these things.
Knowing them doesn't detract from your creativity or spontaneity.
What you're learning isn't a code of ethics or the rules of proper behavior in decent society.
It isn't etiquette or table manners.
You aren't being handcuffed or detained or taught to curtsy
Or forced to wear a borrowed tie at a fancy restaurant
Or compromising your standards.

You're merely learning what is:
The names of the kinds of words, their relation to each other, and their functions.
Like a painter's knowledge of color and the laws of perspective,

A jazz musician's knowledge of chord structures and his instrument.

Your job as a writer is making sentences.
Your other jobs include fixing sentences, killing sentences, and arranging sentences.
If this is the case—making, fixing, killing, arranging—how can your writing possibly flow?
It can't.

Flow is something the reader experiences, not the writer.

A writer may write painstakingly,
Assembling the work slowly, like a mosaic,
Fitting and refitting sentences and paragraphs over the years.
And yet to the reader the writing may seem to flow.

The reader's experience of your prose has nothing to do with how hard or easy it was for you to make.
You're not writing for a reader in the mirror whose psychological state reflects your own.
You have only your own working world to consider.
The reader reads in another world entirely.

So why not give up the idea of "flow" and accept the basic truth about writing?

It's hard work, and it's been hard work for everyone
all along.
There's a good reason to believe this, apart from the
fact that it's true.
If you think that writing—the act of composition—
should flow, and it doesn't, what are you likely to feel?
Obstructed, defeated, inadequate, blocked, perhaps
even stupid.
The idea of writer's block, in its ordinary sense,
Exists largely because of the notion that writing should
flow.

But if you accept that writing is hard work,
And that's what it feels like while you're writing,
Then everything is just as it should be.
Your labor isn't a sign of defeat.
It's a sign of engagement.
The difference is all in your mind, but *what* a difference.

The difficulty of writing isn't a sign of failure.
It's simply the nature of the work itself.

For the writer, the word "flow" is a trap.
So is any word that suggests that writing is a spontaneous emission.
Writing doesn't flow, unless you're plagiarizing or col-
lecting clichés or enlisting volunteer sentences.

You'll experience certain kinds of suddenness as you
work:

The illusion that time is passing quickly,
An episode of unusual mental clarity,
An almost unnoticed transition from one mood to another.

The piece you're working on may take a jump forward,
And you notice the jump instead of the hours and days of thinking that enabled it.
Everything may flow when you're setting thoughts down on paper.
But that's jotting, not writing.

"Flow" means effusion, a spontaneous outpouring of sentences.
But what it really, secretly means is easy writing.

The more you know about making sentences, the easier it is to fix them,
To get out of trouble, to find the really good sentences—
The better sentences—hiding beneath the skin of your thinking.
What matters isn't how fluidly the sentences are emitted.
Only how good they are.

It's easy to believe in "flow" if you can't feel the difference between a dead sentence and a living one
Or see the ambiguities you're accidentally creating.

In other words, "flow" is often a synonym for ignorance and laziness.
It's also a sign of haste, the urge to be done.

Why do I say all this?
Because so many writers worry that their writing isn't
flowing.
They worry that they can't live up to expectations—to
a cultural illusion—
And they get in trouble with themselves because of it.

Don't underestimate how hard it is to discard a cliché
like "flow," even in your own assumptions.
Like so much else about writing well,
Getting rid of useless, even harmful, ideas is hard
work.

———————

What lurks behind "flow"?
Above all, the idea of naturalness.

"Natural" is a word that invites suspicion.
It should always present itself in quotation marks,
A sign that its meaning is slippery.
Humans can justify almost anything by calling it
natural.
Naturalness is the pervasive myth—the one to root out
of your head.

. . .

There's nothing natural about writing except the tendency to assume that it's natural,
Thanks to a false analogy with talking.
The connection between talking and writing is nearly as complex as the connection between reading and writing.

You probably don't remember learning to talk as a child.
You probably do remember learning to shape letters and spell words.
Talking is natural.
Writing is not.
Most children can say words before they're two and speak in sentences before they're three.
They can sing the alphabet song almost as soon as they can sing.
But they can't write the alphabet until they can hold an instrument of writing.
It may seem strange that the manual dexterity needed to hold a pencil—or use a keyboard—comes later than the lingual and mental dexterity needed to speak.
But it does.

In writing, there's always a separateness,
The sense of manipulating a tool for producing words at arm's length,
Out there at the ends of your fingers,
Unlike speaking, which arises invisibly from within, like thought and breath.

In writing, there's a psychological separateness too,
The sense of watching yourself think and thinking
about it as you do,
A self-consciousness that interrupts the movement of
your thoughts
If you experience it while talking.

Humans have a language instinct
But not necessarily a writing instinct.
The difference between talking and writing
Is the difference between breathing and singing well.
It takes years of work to write well,
And only part of that is learning to type.

"Natural," like flow, is also an effect in the reader's
mind.
It doesn't describe the act of writing.
It describes the effect of writing.

And like "flow," "natural" is one of the words behind
writer's block.
So let's suppose there's no such thing as writer's block.
There's loss of confidence
And forgetting to think
And failing to prepare
And not reading enough
And giving up on patience
And hastening to write
And fearing your audience

And never really trying to understand how sentences work.
Above all, there's never learning to trust yourself
Or your capacity to learn or think or perceive.

People will continue to believe that writing is natural.
This harms only writers who believe it themselves.

———————————

And yet good prose often sounds spoken,
As if the writer—or the reader reading aloud—were
saying the sentences.
     (This isn't the same as sounding colloquial.)
But the arc of education—and the arc of emulation—
are usually
Away from spokenness and toward the unspeakable,
Toward longer, more convoluted sentences
Using more elaborate syntax and more jargon-like
diction.

There's nothing natural about making sentences that
sound spoken,
No matter how natural they sound.
What are their characteristics?
They're fairly short.
They're rhythmic, often with the rhythms of actual
speech.
The diction is simple—very few multisyllabic words.

So is the construction—almost no suspended phrases or dependent clauses.
This simplicity makes the rhythm more perceptible.
There's also an acute awareness of the listener's attention and understanding,
A sense of contextual alertness, and a vivid sense of the unspoken.
These are all qualities worth building into your prose.
They must be created, discovered, revealed, constructed.
They don't appear "naturally."

It's always worth asking yourself if you can imagine *saying* a sentence
And adjusting it until you can.
Just as it's always useful to ask yourself, "What *exactly* am I trying to say?"
The answer to that question is often the sentence you need to write down.

When your prose begins to stiffen and your thoughts get stuffy,
It's sometimes worth reworking the piece you're writing as if it were
A letter or a long e-mail to a friend,
Someone who knows you well but hasn't seen you in a while.
What happens?
The prose relaxes, the sentences grow more informal.
You remember to use contractions,

Even the words grow shorter.
Suddenly things are clearer and simpler and more
direct, as if they were being spoken.

But something else happens too.
There's suddenly a wider variety of tone, an emotional
latitude,
A sense that the reader will be able to fill in the gaps,
Even the possibility of humor.

Why the difference?
It isn't the change in genre.
It's the change in the reader.
You're writing to someone who knows you, who
understands your allusions,
Your patterns of speech, who's quick and empathetic
In reading your thoughts and feelings, whether they're
spoken or unspoken.
What makes this reader valuable is a sense of connec-
tion and kinship,
An intuitive grasp of what you say and don't say.

You can make any piece feel like an informal letter
By using the generic characteristics of an informal
letter.
But it's far easier to get that feel
By writing to the reader you imagine reading it.
The reader you construct in your imagination
Changes the way you write almost without your
noticing it.

———————

Behind "flow" there's something else,
Even something ecstatic—
The priority of thoughts over sentences.
Thoughts leaping ahead, words barely keeping up,
A hectic chase.
Or the other way around,
Sentences spinning out of each other, one after the next,
Phrase eliciting phrase, words—if not sentences—rushing ahead of thought.
It feels like inspiration.

We've all had these moments.
They're enticing.
The mistake is overvaluing them.

You have an effusion one day.
It spawns a piece.
As the piece evolves, you try to protect those original, effusive sentences.
Only to realize, at last, that what you're writing won't come together until they've been removed or revised.

What were you trying to protect?
The memory of the excitement you felt when those words "came to you."
        (Where did they "come" from?)

You were protecting the memory of the excitement of really concentrating,
Of paying close attention to your thoughts and, perhaps, your sentences,
The excitement of feeling the galvanic link between language and thought.

That excitement matters, and the memory of it is worth preserving,
Even if those sentences aren't.

Concentration, attention, excitement, will be part of your working state.
Daily.
Flow, inspiration—the spontaneous emission of sentences—will not.
That distinction is worth keeping in mind.

Write consciously, deliberately.
Learn how to get out of trouble.
Learn how to free yourself when you're stuck.
Learn how to know what you're doing when you're making sentences.

The workings of your unconscious mind,
The current of your subterranean thoughts and intuitions,
The flickerings of insight and instinct—
These will always surface, if you write clearly enough to let them.

But they're only some of the tools of your daily work,
Which is making sentences.

The most damaging and obstructive cluster of ideas
you face as a writer are nearly all related to the idea of
"flow."
Like "genius."
And "sincerity."
And "inspiration."

Distrust these words.
They stand for cherished myths, but myths nonetheless.

"Inspiration" is what gets you to the keyboard,
And that's where it leaves you.
Inspiration is about the swift transitions of thought,
Sudden realizations,
Almost all of them carefully prepared for by continu-
ous thinking.
Inspiration has nothing to do with the sustained effort
of making prose.

You'll have many serendipitous moments while
writing.
You'll learn to expect them.
But "inspiration," as it's commonly used, is just another
word for "flow."

———————————

Think of all the requirements writers imagine for themselves:

A cabin in the woods
A plain wooden table
Absolute silence
A favorite pen
A favorite ink
A favorite blank book
A favorite typewriter
A favorite laptop
A favorite writing program
A large advance
A yellow pad
A wastebasket
A shotgun
The early light of morning
The moon at night
A rainy afternoon
A thunderstorm with high winds
The first snow of winter
A cup of coffee in just the right cup
A beer
A mug of green tea
A bourbon
Solitude

Sooner or later the need for any one of these will prevent you from writing.

Anything you think you need in order to write—
Or be "inspired" to write or "get in the mood" to
write—
Becomes a prohibition when it's lacking.
Learn to write anywhere, at any time, in any conditions,
With anything, starting from nowhere.
All you really need is your head, the one indispensable
requirement.

———————

If you consciously shape your writing,
Know its ins and outs, understand its subtleties—
Then you know exactly what you're doing
And are therefore manipulating the reader.
Which, of course, you are.

We hate the thought of being manipulated,
And yet reading means surrendering to the manipula-
tions of the author's prose.
This is an experience we love, love so much, in fact,
That we hope to be able to manipulate readers our-
selves someday.
Readers usually choose not to think of it that way.
They prefer not to think of it at all.
But you should.

One of the few sad parts about writing is that it's
almost impossible to surrender to the manipulation of
your own prose.

(It's just as well.)
What prevents it is the memory of all the choices you've made
Hovering around every sentence you've written.

In writing, it's impossible to express sincerity sincerely.
That is, just by being sincere.
You really mean what you mean to say.
You feel an intense sincerity burning inside you.
And yet your sentences feel choked or formulaic.
Writing can't convey sincerity—or any other emotion or mood in the writer—simply because you feel it.

We believe so strongly in sincerity and naturalness of expression in writing that we're almost unable to see how false this belief is.

If you want the reader to feel your sincerity, your sentences have to enact sincerity—verbally, syntactically, even rhythmically.
They have to reveal the signs of sincerity—a modesty and directness—
Just as you do when you're talking sincerely.

If you speak sincerely with someone
But in a voice and manner that suggest you're being ironic,
Who would believe you're sincere?

. . .

Sincerity is a dramatic role for you and your sentences.
That makes it sound insincere.
But the apparently insincere manipulation of language
is the tool that persuades us of your sincerity.

There is no simple, sincere, "natural" space or role for
you to occupy in your writing.
Writing is always a gesture requiring your dramatic
presence, no matter how subtle—
A presence made up of rhetorical choices:
Choices about who you are in relation to your subject
and your reader,
Choices about your presence in the piece, about diction, structure, and the rigor or casualness with which
your sentences are constructed or linked.

The emotional power the reader feels
Depends on how clearly you know what your words
are doing.
That clarity isn't natural.
It's artificial, the result of hard work.

You be the narrator.
Let *us* be the readers.
You'll discover that being the narrator is not the same
as being yourself.
It's a role, and a dramatic one.
Absorb it and inhabit it.

.   .   .

You're always building a habitation in your prose,
A place from which you speak to the reader.
You're never merely, sincerely yourself.
The question then becomes, who are you?
That's a question every piece needs to answer.

Novelists, short-story writers, and poets understand
the gesture in their writing.
They know they occupy a dramatic role and a rhetorical space.
They're rarely afraid to *be* the narrator or actor, to perform the act of telling a story,
Even if they're telling it under the guise of their own
name.

———————

The sense of who you are, what role you choose to
play,
What gesture you make toward the reader—
These things are far more important than ideas of
"style" or "voice."

Asked to write short sentences, writers often say,
"But what about my style? What will that do to my
voice?"
As if they're sure they have one.
"Style" and "voice" are passive constructs,
Markers of individuality, bow ties of self.

They have more to do with what the writer makes of
himself
Than how the reader experiences his prose.

The idea of "voice" at least implies a notion of dramatic presence,
A sense of the writer's gesture.

But what's a writer's "style"?

Style is an expression of the interest you take in the
making of every sentence.
It emerges, almost without intent, from your engagement with each sentence.
It's the discoveries you make in the making of the prose
itself.

We assume that style is self-expression.
It can be, but only in this sense:
It's the fusion of your command of language and your
commitment to your own intent,
Even as your intent shifts under the weight and
opportunity
Of the discoveries you make as you work,
Discoveries that are linguistic, conceptual, structural,
imaginative.

This doesn't sound like a useful or conventional defini-
tion of style

Or much like self-expression.
But it does clarify an important thought:
"Style" shouldn't linger in your awareness.
You don't need to think about style.
It's as likely to appear in the character of your thinking,
The shape of your ideas, your sense of humor or irony,
As it is in any "stylistic" markers in the prose itself.
But this will only be true if your prose is clear enough
to reveal the character of your thinking, the shape of
your ideas, and your sense of humor or irony.

Where ambiguity rules, there is no "style"—or anything else worth having.

Pursue clarity instead.
In the pursuit of clarity, style reveals itself.
Your clarity will differ from anyone else's without
your intending to make it differ.
Years later, looking back over your collected works,
You can contemplate your style at leisure.
But for now you have more important things to think
about.
Like revision.

———————

All writing is revision.
That's not what you learned in school.
In school you learned to write a draft and then revise.

. . .

But imagine this:
You begin to compose a sentence in your head.
You don't write it down.
You let the sentence play through your mind again.
        (It's only six words long.)
You replace one or two of the words.
You adjust the rhythm by changing the verb.
You discard the metaphor.
You decide you like the sentence.
You write it down.
Is this composition?
Or revision?

It's both.
Composing a sentence always involves revision
Unless you write down the words of a sentence exactly
as they pop into your head.
And why would you do that?

You look at the sentence you've written down.
You choose a simpler noun and a stronger verb.
Is this revision merely because the sentence was already
written down?
Or is it composition too?
It makes no difference.

As it's taught in school, revision means little more than
Correction after the fact

(Or possibly proofreading, a completely forgotten but invaluable skill).
This becomes clear when students ask if they can revise a piece.
They mean can they fix what already exists,
Adjust a sentence here or there,
Move a couple of paragraphs.

They never mean
"Let me reimagine the piece completely,
Beginning with my approach to the subject
And keeping only the handful of sentences that actually worked."

Writers at every level of skill experience the tyranny of what exists.
It can be overwhelming—the inertia of the paragraphs and pages you've already composed, the sentences you've already written,
No matter how rough they are.

Whether you love what you've written or not,
Those sentences have the virtue of already existing,
Which makes them better than sentences that don't exist.
Or so it seems.

And yet because they're rough and provisional,
They form an overlapping grid with unsuspected gaps,
A network that seems to defy revision.

Fixing one sentence almost always means fixing
another and then another
As though revision were an infinitely recursive act.
There's almost never enough time for revision, if revi-
sion comes after the fact
And if it's really revision.

———————

So let's change things.
Try this instead:
Revise at the point of composition.
Compose at the point of revision.
Accept no provisional sentences.
Make no drafts
And no draft sentences.
Bring the sentence you're working on as close to its
final state as you can
Before you write it down and after.
Do the same for the next sentence
And right on through to the end.
Think of composition and revision as the same thing,
Different versions of thinking,
Philosophically indistinguishable.

The usual premise is that composition brings something new to the page
And revision fixes it.
This is a useless distinction, and it creates a false sense
of priority—

A belief that the writer's real work is making newness out of nothing,
As if creativity only takes place where the ink stops and the blank page begins,
Where the cursor sits blinking.
As if newness couldn't originate between sentences or within a sentence.
As if revision were essentially secondary and uncreative.

Revision (or composition) just as often means
Writing from the middle—from the many middles—and not the end.
The end—where the page goes blank—has no priority.
You're not reading, picking up where you left off.
You're writing.
You left off everywhere at once.
You may have left off in the middle of a paragraph many pages ago,
And everything since has been a detour.
You may find the path you're looking for only by taking a detour.
As you begin rereading a piece you're working on,
Don't hurry to resume work at the end.
Treat every sentence you read as if it were still under revision.

Composing and revising at the same time won't be easy at first.
You'll make sentences that seem finished and then find flaws in them.

Finding flaws is how you learn to make better sentences.
Enjoy it.
You can't prevent yourself from repeating a mistake
you haven't noticed.
You'll have to read your work many, many times to
find all the problems embedded in it.
Even experienced writers have to do this.
Some flaws do a wonderful job of hiding.

So, you'll be revising each sentence as you compose it.
Composing each sentence as you revise it.
And you'll read and reread every sentence you make
many dozens of times,
Sifting out problems as they materialize in front of
you.
You'll be looking for flaws.
But also for opportunities—and for missed oppor-
tunities:
Things you might have said, ideas you might have
developed,
Connections you might have made.

Revision isn't only the act of composition.
Revision is thinking applied to language,
An opening and reopening of discovery,
A search for the sentence that says the thing you had no
idea you could say
Hidden inside the sentence you're making.

.   .   .

Revision is the writer's reading,
The habit of noticing choices,
Noticing that every sentence might be otherwise but
isn't.

———————————

Language writhes with urgency to be saying something.
Your job is to understand and control that urgency.

At first, what you mean to say will emerge
By setting aside the things you don't mean to say
As well as trying to say the thing itself.

Learning to do this will take some time.
You'll feel as though you've bogged down,
As though you'll never find your way to the end.
But you'll also find yourself making discoveries you
never could have predicted,
Finding thoughts you never knew existed because they
didn't exist
Until you were exploring sentences for their implicit
possibilities.

With practice, this will become a more efficient and
more creative way to write,
A way of discovering what you didn't know you could
say,

Which also means learning something important about
yourself.

It's also a vastly more interesting way to write.
With practice, it will become more efficient in every
sense,
Faster, more accurate, and far more direct than the way
you were taught to write.
You'll learn to trust it implicitly
And yourself as well.

Where do sentences come from?
How do they reveal themselves in your thinking?
We like to think we move from thought to expression,
With no more fuss than a handshake.

Sometimes you know just what you want to say,
And you find the words to say exactly that.
But just as often what you want to say emerges as the
sentence takes shape.
The thought isn't primary or absolute.
The thought is only a hint.
Language offers guidance and resistance both.
The sentence *becomes* the thought by bringing it fully
into being.
We assume that thought shapes the sentence.
But thought and sentence are always a collaboration,
The sum of what can be said and what you're trying
to say.

. . .

In writing you love, the sentences are endlessly various.
How do you find that variety in your own prose?
One way is by looking for sameness, uniformity, and working against it.
You wouldn't repeat the same words over and over again,
So why repeat so many sentence structures?
Better to look for that variety as you're thinking and writing,
Giving as much attention to the shape of the sentence
As you do to what you're trying to say.

Sometimes a rhythm insinuates itself.
You find yourself listening for echoes, opportunities.
Sometimes you find yourself watching the traces of words,
Phrases, memories, flitting through your mind.
Each of these can engender a sentence, offer a shape.
Be responsive to the variations that present themselves as you think.

Soon, you'll grasp that sentences originate and take their endless variety
From within you, from your reading,
Your tactile memory for rhythms,
Your sense of the playfulness at the heart of the language,
Your perception of the world.

· · ·

You'll learn to let a single word, a simple rhythm,
A thing you've noticed,
Generate a sentence you didn't expect.
This requires a change in your mental habits.
And a reconsideration of how you work.

———————

In the outline and draft model of writing, thinking is
largely done up front.
Outlining means organizing the sequence of your
meanings, not your sentences.
It derogates the making of sentences.
It ignores the suddenness of thought,
The surprises to be found in the making of sentences.
It knows nothing of the thoughtfulness you'll discover
as you work.

It prevents discovery within the act of writing.
It says, planning is one thing, writing another,
And discovery has nothing to do with it.
It overemphasizes logic and chronology
Because they offer apparently "natural" structures.
It preserves the cohesiveness of your research
And leaves you with a heap of provisional sentences,
Which are supposed to sketch the thoughts you've
already outlined.

· · ·

It fails to realize that writing comes from writing.

You're more likely to find the right path—
The interesting path through your subject and thoughts—
In a sentence-by-sentence search than in an outline.

The standard model wastes the contemplative space of writing.
Can you think all the good thoughts in advance?

Outlining has at least as much to do with rescuing the writer from himself
As it does with planning the shape of the piece.
It's meant to free you from thinking as you write.
It provides a catwalk across the open spaces in your mind
To keep you from falling into rumination as you write.
You'll never know what you think until you escape your outline.

The purpose of an outline is also to conserve your material, to distribute it evenly so that *meaning* discloses itself near the end.

Here's a better approach.
Squander your material.
Don't ration it, saving the best for last.
You don't know what the best is.
Or the last.

Use it up.
There's plenty more where that came from.
You won't make new discoveries until you need them.

What writers fear most is running out of material.
The sound of a writer's fears is the sound of nothing—
No typing, no clicking, no scratching of pens.
But you can only run out of material
If you haven't been thinking or noticing.

Try this:
No outline.
Research, reading, noticing, interviewing, traveling,
paying attention, note taking—all the work you do to
understand the subject, whatever it is, whatever kind
of piece you're writing.
Reread your notes, and take notes on them.
And again.
Take notes on your thoughts.
Most of all, take notes on what *interests* you.
Be certain you've marked out what *interests* you.
Don't make an outline from your notes.
Don't turn your notes into a road map for the sentences
to come.

Reread your notes.
No matter how long or short they are.

.   .   .

Then think.
And think again.
Learn to be patient in the presence of your thoughts.
Learn to be equally patient in the presence of a new
sentence or a phrase you like.
Let yourself pause and work on that sentence.
In your head.
Don't write it down.
Be patient.
Pay attention to everything you're thinking.
Notice your thoughts,
See if you can feel your awareness illuminating them.

If you're paying attention, you'll notice that some of
your thoughts interest you and some don't.
How can you tell?
You'll stop and rethink the thought,
Pause in its presence.

Let the thoughts that interest you distract you.
Ask yourself about them.
Why do they interest you?
What were you thinking about before they appeared?
Then come back to the main sequence,
Unless you've discovered a better main sequence
By following a thought you're interested in.

Don't try to distinguish between thinking and making
sentences.
Pretend they're the same thing.

Don't rush your thinking.
Don't rush to make sentences.
See what happens when you try to put words to a
thought that interests you.
See what words the thought itself is presenting and try
making a sentence out of them,
A sentence like the ones we've been talking about, with
rhythm and clarity and balance.
Not a volunteer sentence.
See if the thought you're interested in becomes sharper
and clearer by making a sentence from it.
It may become more obscure.
What does that tell you?
Don't panic, keep working at it.

If you make a sentence while thinking,
It doesn't mean you have to make more sentences
immediately.
You can go back to thinking and see what the business
of making a sentence stirred up in you.
It may have dislodged other thoughts, other connections.

No one will teach you how to wait while you think or
what to wait for while you're thinking.
You'll have to teach yourself.
Above all, you'll have to teach yourself to be patient.

.   .   .

Trying this once or twice won't do.

It's a skill, not an instinct.

You may have to try it in small increments,

And you may have to cling to a partial outline for a while.

That's okay,

As long as you're prepared to abandon it.

It's a map of the places you may end up not going.

Practice,

And you'll learn to trust the agility and capacity of your thinking.

You'll learn that you don't have to set aside inviolate chunks of time to think.

You'll find yourself working—thinking, making sentences—in the brief intervals of your ordinary life,

In increments no longer than a few seconds.

How long does a thought take?

Or a sentence?

Your thinking will help you discover what interests you in the subject you've chosen

No matter how indirectly or elliptically or obliquely connected it is.

Any thread, any perception, any link, any phrase, any intuition.

You may discover an orderly way to go about this,

Or you may move through your thoughts in ways you can't predict.

It makes no difference.
Resist the temptation to start organizing and structur-
ing your thoughts too soon,
Boxing them in, forcing them into genre-sized
containers.
Postpone the search for order, for the single line
through the piece.
Let your thoughts overlap and collide and see what
they dislodge.

How do you begin to write?
Look for a sentence that interests you.
A sentence that might begin the piece.
Don't look too hard.
Just try out some sentences.
Lots of them.
See how they sound.
Do any of them sound first?
Discard them readily, easily, with no sense of loss,
Then try out some more.
This is important.
Get used to discarding sentences.

You're holding an audition.
Many sentences will try out.
One gets the part.
You'll recognize it less from the character of the sen-
tence itself

than from the promise it contains—promise for the sentences to come.

This will get easier with practice.
Don't be alarmed if it takes a day or two of trying out sentences
Before you find the promising one.
It may only be promising enough to lead you to the real first sentence.

Be casual about this.
Look for a sentence that interests you,
A sentence whose possibilities you like because of the potential you see in its wake.
I don't mean a "fantastic first sentence" or one that sounds "introductory."

I don't mean a sentence that sounds first because it sounds like other first sentences you've read.
I don't mean the kind of first sentence teachers sometimes talk about—the one that *grabs* the reader.
The reader doesn't need grabbing.
She needs to feel your interest in the sentence you've chosen to make.
Nothing more.

What makes the first sentence interesting?
Its exact shape and what it says
And the possibility it creates for another sentence.

. . .

A beginning needs no éclat, no cleverness, no tricks,
No coyly hidden awareness of where the piece will take us.
The opening sentence is only creating an opening for the next sentence.

But there's also nothing incidental about that first sentence.
You—your role as a writer, the role you construct, your presence to the reader—you and your first sentence begin together.

You want to *begin* the piece, not *introduce* it, which is the difference between a first sentence already moving at speed and a first sentence that wants to generalize while clearing its throat.

The beginning is one sentence long.
It leads to the next sentence and is largely indistinguishable from other sentences leading to the next sentence.
So many writers stumble by making the first sentence try to do too much
And end up making every sentence try to do the same.

Out of all the possibilities created by the first sentence,
Make a second sentence, full of more possibilities, even disconnected ones.

See if you can write the sentence that *arises* from the first sentence,

Not the sentence that *follows* from it,

Even if that means the second sentence lies at some distance from the first.

The second sentence you write may turn out

Not to be the second sentence after all.

It may be the ninth.

The sentence isn't burdened by the question, where will it go?

The piece is now two sentences long.

Not two sentences plus the missing pages that haunt you.

The next step is to make the piece three sentences long.

Don't worry about trajectory or sequence.

Don't look further ahead than two or three sentences.

And don't *plan* those sentences.

Write them in your head instead.

Resist the temptation to rush ahead to see where they're pointing.

What matters isn't where they're pointing

But what interests you in the sentence you're making,

Which you may have to discover as you make it.

Don't steer the sentences where you want them to go.

See if you can follow them there.

They may be going in many different directions at first.

. . .

Don't get trapped by the thought of writing sequentially.
If you uncover a sentence that seems to belong to an
earlier passage,
Go back to that passage and work there.

You have no idea what you're going to say
Until you discover what you want to say
As you make the sentences that say it.
Every sentence is optional until it proves otherwise.
Writing is the work of discovery.

Imagine sentences instead of writing them.
Keep them imaginary until you're happy with them.
An imaginary sentence somehow feels less *bound* than
one you've written down.
Making sentences soon ceases to be a separate act
And becomes part of the process of thinking.
Aren't you already thinking in sentences?

You'll discover that the act of making sentences in
your head—
Composing and revising at the same time,
Making them sharper and more accurate—
Tends to uncover thoughts you didn't know you had,
Allowing you to say things you didn't know you knew
how to say
In sentences stronger than you knew you could make.

. . .

Soon you find yourself *expecting* to say things you didn't know you knew how to say.

You'll get into the habit of surprising yourself.

The reader will feel the freshness of the discovery in the prose

Because the writer almost always reveals the excitement of making a discovery

In the rhythm and the vividness of the sentences themselves.

But you distrust your memory.

You're afraid you'll forget the sentences you're imagining.

Why would you?

They're important.

Write them down, just in case.

And then go back to thinking—imagining sentences and their possibilities,

Feeling your way into each new opportunity.

But imagine the sentence in its entirety—and the next one too—before writing anything down.

Sit back from the keyboard or notepad.

Sit back, and continue to think.

That's where the work gets done.

.   .   .

You may glimpse where the piece might go.
You may even see your way through to the end.
If you do, you'll feel a fresh anxiety about forgetting,
As if the forest were closing in on the path you see before you can reach
The warm, welcoming cottage where writing is over.
But thought isn't as fleeting as you think, nor does it come completely unbidden.
If the thought was worth having, you'll rediscover it or find a better one.
The fear of forgetting and the rush to be done are closely related.

You'll learn to trust your memory as you work,
Though it isn't even a matter of trusting your memory.
You'll realize that thinking and remembering are almost indistinguishable.
You're not only imagining sentences you want to write down.
You're also reexploring your subject, sifting your research
And all the elements that make up your subject
Even as you're imagining sentences.
Soon the distinction between thinking about your subject and
Thinking about sentences vanishes.

You'll have stopped making sentences in quarantine,
In the special ward set aside for sentence making once the outline is finished,

The way you were taught in school.
Instead, writing becomes intrinsic to the act of thinking,
Completely intertwined with it.

You're also learning to trust the ability to work in your head
And learning how your mind works,
Which is something you may not have noticed before.

We're always hastening to be done writing,
But we're also hastening to get out of the presence of our thoughts.
Everything about thinking makes us nervous.
We don't believe there's much of value to be found there.
We don't know when we'll come to the end of our thoughts,
But we think it may be soon.

Why?

Your mind is silent yet filled with voices and uncertainty.
The uncertainty you feel is one of the places sentences will come from,
And experience will make your uncertainty more certain.

Stop fearing what you'll find as you think.

Give yourself over to this experiment.
Your intentions will diverge from themselves.
Your starting point may lead to places you didn't imagine,
Places that ask you to reconsider your starting point.
You may feel yourself clinging to your original intention.
Why?
Because it came first?
Why not follow the crosscurrents of your thinking
And see where they lead?
I don't mean follow them blindly.
Allow your thinking to adjust your intentions in the light of your discoveries.
This may mean relinquishing your original intention
If you find a better one as you write.

The piece you're writing is simply the one that happens to get written.
If you'd begun another way, made a different turn, even started in a different mood,
A different piece would have come into being.
The writer's world is full of parallel universes.
You discover, word by word, the one you discover.
Ten minutes later—another hour of thought—and you would have found your way into a different universe.
The piece is permeable to the world around it.

It's responsive to time itself, to the very hour of its creation.

This is an immensely freeing thing to understand.

It liberates you from the anxiety of sequence,
The fear that there's only one way through your subject,
Only one useful approach.

Learn to accept the discontinuity between yourself and what you write,
The discontinuity between your will, your intention, your plan
And the discoveries you make as you work.

Abandon the idea of predetermination,
The shaping force of your intention,
Until you've given it up for good.
Bring your intentions, by all means, but accept that the language we use
Is a language of accidentals, always skewing away from the course we set.
This is something not to mourn but to revel in—
Not only for the friction and sideslip inherent in the language
But for freeing us from the narrowness of our preconceptions.

.   .   .

Imagine this:

The piece you're writing is about what you find in the piece you're writing.

Nothing else.

No matter how factual, how nonfictional, how purposeful a piece it is.

Sooner or later, you'll become more interested in what you're able to say on the page and less interested in your intentions.

You'll rely less on the priority of your intentions and more on the immediacy of writing.

It may sound as if I'm describing a formless sort of writing.

Not at all.

Form is discovery too.

It's perfectly possible to write this way even when constricted by

A narrow subject, a small space, and a tight deadline.

How do you decide what works?

What do you do when your sentences seem to waver in quality and value before your eyes?

You read what you've written, and it looks good.

You read it again, and it looks bad.

You read it a third time, and now you can't tell.

Your emerging skill as a reader will help.

You'll read your sentences against the backdrop of all the rest of your reading.

You'll get better at examining your own choices—the ones you've already made

And the ones you see waiting to be made as you reread what you've written.

Before long you'll notice possibilities you would have been blind to once upon a time.

You'll see that some of your sentences are still conjectural.

You'll stop seeing only the narrow procession of the sentences you've made

And start noticing the thoughts and implications surrounding them.

You'll become strangely aware of what you've chosen not to say

And how that affects the sound of your sentences.

Writers too often respond to whole chunks of what they've written,

Whether it's a paragraph or the entire piece.

You read it and think, "This is terrible," and throw the whole thing away with a sinking heart.

You read it and think, "This is terrific," with a smile and set it aside, done.

Both responses end your engagement with what you've written.

There's a better way.

Start by fixing the sentences that need fixing.

(There will surely be some. If you can't find any, look harder, or begin rereading this book.)

Explore the possibilities that open up.
Continue making small, incremental changes
At the sentence level wherever you see problems,
With no priority given to the beginning or end of the
piece.
Listen for rhythm.

Keep reading and rereading what you've written.
Anything that strikes you—anything that causes a
subtle, inward sensation of discomfort, an inner alarm,
no matter how faint—stop there and figure out what's
going on.
It may have to do not with the sentence itself
But with its relation to some other sentence.
There's no rush.

It's surprising where these incremental changes lead,
How they solidify what seems to be unstable,
How they open up directions you hadn't glimpsed
before.
You may find that the most important section of the
piece—a section you haven't written yet—emerges
from the gap created when you break a long sentence
in two.

It's true that the simplest revision is deletion.
But there's often a fine sentence lurking within a bad
sentence,
A better sentence hiding under a good sentence.

Work word by word until you discover it.

Don't try to fix an existing sentence with minimal effort,

Without reimagining it.

You can almost never fix a sentence—

Or find the better sentence within it—

By using only the words it already contains.

If they were the right words already, the sentence probably wouldn't need fixing.

And yet writers sit staring at a flawed sentence as if it were a Rubik's Cube,

Trying to shift the same words round and round until they find the solution.

Take note of this point: it will save you a lot of frustration.

This applies to paragraphs too.

You may not be able to fix the paragraph using only the sentences it already contains.

How soon will you be getting good?

Why not ask how soon you'll be getting clear?

Look for improvement wherever you find it,

And build on every improvement.

But don't look for too much improvement all at once.

Finding a flaw is an improvement.

So is discarding an unnecessary word or using a stronger verb.

Writing even one clear, balanced, rhythmic sentence is an accomplishment.

It prepares the way for more good sentences.
It teaches you how you respond, inwardly, to a successful sentence of your own making.

If you write a good sentence, how will you know it's good?
You may *know* it's good, feel certain about it.
But you're likelier to sense an inward difference,
A subtle feeling telling you this sentence isn't the same as the others.
Even beginning writers notice this.
Learning that feeling is important.
It's a guide and an incentive to making more good sentences.

This doesn't happen in a void.
It happens against the backdrop of your constant reading,
Your unending exposure to superb sentences.

And then one day
You'll write a sentence that says more than its words alone can say.
You'll know that it says what you mean without having said it,
And you'll know that the reader knows it too.
This will sound impossible until you've done it once.
Then you'll see how possible it is, and how inviting.
It lets the reader complete the thought.

It sets an echo in motion.
This is writing by implication.

Don't let the success of a sentence or a paragraph or a piece deter you.
Some writers freeze, fearing the next one won't be as good.
Some writers polish a single paragraph until it glows,
Fearing that the next paragraph will ruin it somehow.
Accept it: you'll surely fail again and just as surely succeed.
There's nothing linear or steady in your growth as a writer.
And the moment you find yourself getting good at one thing,
It's time to push on into unsafe terrain.

To do this work requires a balance between your commitment to the sentences you're making
And the knowledge that each of them could be otherwise.
Some should be otherwise; some shouldn't.
Make that simple distinction again and again
And you'll get good at making that simple distinction,
Which is the foundation of writing.
You'll learn to live somewhere between certainty and flux.

You'll learn to remember that your sentences don't acquire their final inertia
Until *you* release them.

There's nothing permanent in the state of being written down.
Your sentences, written down, are in the condition of waiting to be examined.

You commit yourself to each sentence as you make it,
And to each sentence as you fix it,
Retaining the capacity to change everything and
Always remembering to work from the small-scale—
The scale of the sentence—upward.

Rejoicing and despair aren't very good tools for revising.
Curiosity, patience, and the ability to improvise are.
So is the ability to remain open to the work and let it remain open to you.

———————

Don't confuse order with linearity.
You'll find more than enough order in the thoughts and sentences that interest you.
By order I mean merely connections—
Some close, some oblique, some elliptical—
Order of any kind you choose to create, any way you choose to move.

. . .

Don't give in to the memory of your school writing,
The claustrophobic feeling that there's only one right
order of arguing, proving, demonstrating,
The assumption that logic persuades the reader
Instead of the clarity of what you're saying.

There's little actual logic in good writing.
There's a current of thoughts and ideas and observations.
Some may be linked by evidence.
One point may substantiate or corroborate another.
But what passes for logic or argument is usually little
more than a succession of ideas
Connected mostly by proximity and analogy.

Writing doesn't prove anything,
And it only rarely persuades.
It does something much better.
It attests.
It witnesses.
It shares your interest in what you've noticed.
It reports on the nature of your attention.
It suggests the possibilities of the world around you.
The evidence of the world as it presents itself to you.

Proof is for mathematicians.
Logic is for philosophers.
We have testimony.

. . .

The logic of writing, as you learned it in school,
Turns out to mean little more than an obsession with transition
And the scattering of rhetorical tics—overused, nearly meaningless words and phrases.

In fact.
Indeed.
On the one hand.
On the other hand.
Therefore.
Moreover.
However.
In one respect.
Of course.
Whereas.
Thus.

These are logical indicators. Emphasizers. Intensifiers.
They insist upon logic whether it exists or not.
They often come first in the sentence,
Trying to steer the reader's understanding from the front,
As if the reader were incapable of following a logical shift in the middle of the sentence,
As if the sentence had been written in the order the writer thought of the words,
Without any reconsideration.
These words take the reader's head between their hands and force her to look where they want her to.

Imagine how obnoxious that is,
That persistent effort to predetermine and overgovern
the reader's response.

These phrases also obscure the content of your
sentences.
If a piece is truly assured in its order, no matter how
connected or oblique,
It needs no logical indicators.
It will be obvious when one sentence negates or affirms
another.

These words betray the writer's anxiety,
The false belief that proof is necessary and possible,
That persuasion is just a "thus" away.
They also try to bolster the apparent authority of your
piece
By echoing the apparent authority of other people
Who can't write and who distrust their own thinking.

A simple experiment:
Try removing "but" wherever you can,
And see if the sense of negation or contradiction—
The feel of a reversal taking place—isn't still present.
"But" is always preferable to "however,"
Except in the rare cases where "however" is preferable
to "but,"
Which has everything to do with rhythm, formality,
and context.
And yes, you may begin a sentence with "but."

Another example of linearity: chronology.
Chronology will always offer itself as the "natural"
means of telling a story or recounting an event.
But there's nothing "natural" about moving chrono-
logically in writing.
It's a rhetorical choice among many choices, and usu-
ally a dull one at that.
It feels like a privileged choice only by analogy with
the sequence of our own lives.
Chronology in our lives is "natural" in a limited sense.
We live on time's arrow,
And our days and nights follow the clock.
But there's no such thing as thought's arrow
Or mood's arrow
Or memory's arrow.

Consider your interior life—what you feel and think
and the ways you remember.
How much of it is chronological in order?
Brief segments may be imbued with the orderliness of
time.
But in their relation to each other the elements of our
internal lives are more likely to be associative, even
dissociative,
Linked in ways that have nothing to do with the clock
or the day by day of life itself.
Writing is often an appeal not to the order of our
chronological lives

But to the order of our internal lives,
Which is nonchronological and, in fact, unorderly.

Resist chronology.
It will always try to impose itself.
Break the flow of time once it begins.
Better yet, resist it from the start.
If there's a pleasure in seeing time revealed as we read,
There's an equal pleasure in seeing it suspended, violated,
And broken as only writing can do.
Use the simple past tense—
Avoiding the layering of several pasts—
And give the reader clear temporal clues when needed.

It takes a skillful writer to make the ordinary motion of time engaging.
Narrative is harder to write than almost anything else.
Novels contain far less chronological narrative than you think.
Take a page from almost any novelist.
Look carefully at each sentence.
How many propel the story forward in time?
And how many are devoted to enriching our sense of place and character?

Our lives are full of endings.
The sun goes down every day.
We ask for the check.

Eventually it comes.
How broad a hint does it take to make a reader who
lives on a planet full of endings
Feel the end of your piece approaching?
You've already written the ending you need.
You didn't see it, because you were looking for some-
thing more dramatic.
The reader saw the end coming from miles away.

When I say resist chronology, I also mean resist the
chronology of observation.
Why report on events in the order you observed them?
Why stick to the sequence in which things happened
Unless there's a good reason for it?
I also mean the chronology of the evidence you gather,
The way it tends to clump together in your notes and
pieces,
Lumps of this and lumps of that as if every word
Adhered stickily to a cohort of equally sticky words:
The transcript of the interview, the quotation from an
article,
The sequence of your impressions as you arrive on the
scene.

Your job isn't to arrange chunks of evidence,
Chunks of the world in the order you gather them.
Your job is to *atomize* everything you touch,
To dissect your evidence into its details and particu-
lars and

Resist the inherent jargon of your subject,
Breaking apart every clod of words you come across.
Your job is to undo the adhesiveness of the evidence you've gathered,
Its tendency to clump into indissoluble units.
Dissolve them.
Pay attention only to what interests you in it.
Break the complexity of what you've learned into the very small pieces of a mosaic
Shaped not by the clumping of evidence but by your conscious decisions as a writer.
Use the one detail you need as you need it.
Beware of the way it sticks to other details.
Why reproduce the whole scene when only one moment matters?
Use only the quotation you need where you think it belongs,
And only the very bit that matters.
Use only the words *you* choose.

Writing is a way of ordering perception, but it's just as often a reordering of perception in a form peculiar to the writer's discovery.
Telling takes the order *you* want it to, which may have nothing to do with the order that seems "natural," the order that volunteers itself.

The order of what you're writing is determined by your interest in the material

And the sense you make of it and by your presence to the reader.
You're not just filling space now.

––––––––––

Here's an experiment:
Copy or print out a couple of pages from a nonfiction work you admire, something not purely memoir.
(For example, the opening of Truman Capote's *In Cold Blood*.)
Underline each fact or assertion, every detail of landscape or character or time or causation.
Remember that everything you're reading—
The very scene in your mind that emerges from the page—
Is a construct of assembled facts.
Then ask yourself, how does the author know these things?

See if you can imagine, or guess, the source of his evidence for each detail,
Each quotation, the particles of every description.
Make a list of those sources.
I don't mean merely the books and articles the author may have read.
I mean people interviewed, repeated visits to the site
On days when the weather differed in different seasons.
I mean police logs and newspapers, hearsay and rumor,

County records and tax rolls, photo albums and
gravestones,
Anything the author might have touched upon to
make these pages.

It adds up to quite a collection,
From which the author has taken, bit by bit, only the
elements he wants.
The evidence has been atomized.
Each minute detail has been removed from the imme-
diate neighborhood of
Its original context—where it was first found or
noticed or transcribed—
And given a new neighborhood in the web of the prose
itself,
Where newly autonomous facts surround it,
Each of them relocated too.

This new neighborhood is governed by many forces,
including rhythm.
Above all, it's governed by the writer's needs.
Not by chronology or logic or spatial sequence
Or any other organization that seems, at first glance, to
be "natural."
There will be moments of chronology,
Moments of analysis and reflection,
Moments of visual movement,
Like a tracking shot in the movies.
There will be moments of stationary depth,

Like a landscape drawing by Rembrandt.
But the order of the piece is not determined by any
single one of them.
It can have many orders, all flowing into one,
Which is the reader's experience.

———————

You were taught in school to repose on the authority
of the evidence you gathered,
The resplendent figures you quoted.
You remember those papers, filled with great lumps of
quotation.
Your sentences piloted around them like a ship among
icebergs.

But what if you were to muster your own authority?
I don't mean making up facts and quotations.
I mean, what if the reader trusted your prose,
Listened with interest to what you're saying
For the sake of what you're saying,
Instead of noting the complacency, the deference, even
the ceremony
With which you bow to the authorities you cite?

What if the reader believed, somehow, in you?
Listened for your voice, not the voices of others?
Watched for your perceptions?
What if the reader felt your authority
And thought about quoting *you*?

. . .

In our world—the writing world—
Authority always rests in the hands of the reader,
Who can simply close the book and choose another.
The most fashionable novels and the greatest poems
Cannot force you to read themselves.
Authority always belongs to the reader.

A reader who's opened a book to its first page is in a tender predicament,
Whether she's standing in the aisle of a bookstore or sitting at home.
All the authority belongs to her—the authority to close the book.
And yet she's willing—yearning—to surrender her authority to the author
And keep reading.

Readers exercise their authority almost unconsciously
In their search for the authority that belongs to the author.

As a reader, you know the feeling of looking up after eighty pages and wondering how you got there,
The sense of immersion, of entering a shared but private space.

All the authority a writer ever possesses is the authority the reader grants him.

Yet the reader grants it in response to her sense of the writer's authority.

Authority arises only from clarity of language and clarity of perception.
Authority is how the reader's trust is engaged.

"Authority" is another word for the implicit bond between writer and reader,
The desire to keep reading.
The desire to follow the writer wherever she goes.
The question isn't, can the reader follow you?
That's a matter of grammar and syntax.
The question is, will the reader follow you?

———————

You've been told again and again that you have to seduce the reader,
Sell the story in the very first paragraph.
      (Nonsense, but it explains a lot of bad writing.)
The reader isn't looking for the tease of a single paragraph,
Or numbingly clever prose, or sentences full of self-exhibition.
The reader is in love with continuity, with extent, with duration,
Above all with presence—the feeling that each sentence isn't merely a static construct but *inhabited* by the writer.

Examine yourself while reading and see if that isn't true.

Rhythm is a vital source of the writer's authority.
If the sentences were shaped any other way, the rhythm would be completely different.
Rhythm comes to the reader as a precursor of many things.
It anticipates the intelligibility of the sentence.
It grounds the tongue and the mind.
It creates balance and propulsion.
It's deeply assuring and worth getting right.

Most of all:
Authority arises from the way you write,
Not from the subject you write about.
No subject is so good that it can redeem indifferent writing.
But good writing can make almost any subject interesting.
That's the point of my epigraph from Joyce Carol Oates:
"The subject is *there* only by the grace of the author's language."
Your grace, your authority, doesn't borrow the subject's validity:
It creates it.

The subject can never justify your prose or redeem its failures.

When it comes to writing, the intensity of the writer's feelings and
The power of the subject mean almost nothing.
We only glimpse that power and intensity
In the power and intensity of the prose.

Yet somehow we believe that subject is everything.
We believe the writer *is* her story
And that her authority somehow depends on what's happened in her life,
That her authority is authenticity.
People clamor to tell their stories in words.
This doesn't make them writers,
Nor does it make their stories matter.

If *you* are your story, where do you get another?

If you understand how to build silence and patience and clarity into your prose,
How to construct sentences that are limber and rhythmic and precise
And filled with perception,
You can write about anything, even yourself.

You may feel uncomfortable with the word
"authority."
Perhaps it sounds dominant, overbearing, "authoritarian." You may need to work on the problem of
self-deprecation,
Self-distrust,
Especially when it comes to noticing the world around
you
And what you're able to say about it.
You may be used to denying your perceptions and dismissing your awareness.
You may be caught in a constant state of demurral
Or have the habit of belittling yourself.

Watch for the chronic language of self-disparagement,
The moments when you say, "My problem is . . ."
Or "It doesn't matter what I think."
If you say these kinds of things, you probably say them
out of habit, almost unconsciously.
This is a product of your education too, at home and
at school.
Pay attention to it.
Recognize how harmful it is.
Its message—subliminal and overt—is that your perceptions are worthless.

Do everything you can to subvert this habit.

.   .   .

The most subversive thing you can do is to write
clearly and directly,
Asserting the facts as you understand them,
Your perceptions as you've gathered them.

You'll ground your own authority in the language
itself
As your sentences become better and better.
You may need to write for yourself for a while,
And listen only to the language.
That's okay.
The first person who needs to be persuaded of your
authority
Is you.
Don't make it impossible to persuade yourself.

Part of the trouble may be this:
You're afraid your ideas aren't good enough,
Your sentences not clever or original enough.

But what if your ideas are coherent and thoughtful?
What if your perceptions are accurate and true?
Your sentences clear and direct?
What if allowing us to see what's accurate and true is
among the best work writing can do?
Saying the obvious thing briefly and clearly and
Observing the critical detail are hard enough.

It's surprising how often ideas that seem obvious to you
Are in no way apparent to the reader.

And vice versa.

What seems like common sense to you may come as a revelation to the reader.

The only sure test of your ideas is whether they interest you

And arouse your own expectations—

The capacity for surprise that you discover as you work.

One purpose of writing—its central purpose—is to offer your testimony

About the character of existence at this moment.

It will be part of your job to say how things are,

To attest to life as it is.

This will feel strange at first.

You'll wonder whether you're allowed to say things that sound

Not merely observant but true,

And not only true in carefully framed, limited circumstances,

But true for all of us and, perhaps, for all time.

Who asked you to say how things are?

Where do you get the authority to do any of this?

The answer is yours to find.

———————

Some people think that discipline is imposed from without,

Regular hours, strict containment, rigorous exclusion.

Some people think discipline is revealed from within,
Enlightenment, purity, solidity of intent.

Discipline is nothing more than interest and expecta-
tion, a looking forward.
It's never hard to work when you're interested in what
you're working on.

But what if you hate what you're working on?
It helps to examine the content of your loathing.
What is it you hate?
The movement of your ideas?
The nature of your prose?
The obligations and prohibitions you still secretly
honor?
The rules and fears you cling to?

Does it feel as though every word you set down is part
of an inescapable trap?
As though you're following a logic or order that's not
your own?
Building a maze with nothing but dead ends?
Writing in a language you would never say?

It's surprising how often the trouble with a piece of
writing
Has nothing to do with the writing itself.
The trouble is anything that keeps you from looking
with undiverted attention at what you're thinking and
trying to say,

At how you're trying to say it and what the sentence is revealing.
Anything that keeps you from watching the foreground of your mind.

True discipline is remembering and recovering— inventing if necessary—what interests *you*.
If it doesn't interest *you,* how could it possibly interest anyone else?

———————

The problem may not be the sentences at all.
It may be the expectations that seem to emerge as you write,
The different audiences you're trying to please,
The criticisms you imagine,
The conventions you're obeying without actually choosing them,
The constraints of genre,
Not to mention an endless army of volunteer sentences.

Are you writing on a truly blank screen or piece of paper?
Or are you writing on a palimpsest of rules and regulations,
Things you think you must do, methods you must conform to?

.   .   .

Make yourself aware of the forces getting in the way
of your writing.

You may be creating syntactical and logical patterns
that cast themselves forward
Into future sentences and end up constricting you.
Parallelisms and contrasts, for instance.
They seem to offer structure and guidance, but they're
tying your hands.
Notice how instinctively you grasp any pattern, any
parallel,
Any connection that promises to help you define how
The next few sentences, the next few paragraphs, will
lay themselves out.
It's as though you can't help wanting the piece to move
faster or seem easier to write.
Resist that instinct.

You'll recognize the feeling when that happens, the
sense of being trapped,
Coerced into writing a sentence of a predetermined
shape.

One of the most powerful feelings a writer experiences
while working
Is a sense of obligation, of *having* to make a sentence or
a paragraph
This way or that way, being obliged to write *that* sentence or *that* paragraph.

It's a terrible feeling and always a sign of trouble.
Question that obligation. See if you can think your way around it.

Avoiding what you feel you *must* write is as much a part of writing
As discovering what you didn't know you could write.
Every sentence is entitled to structural freedom.

Yet part of the writer's economy is sometimes finding
The simplest, most direct route, making a simpler, plainer sentence,
Accepting that in the variety of sentences you make,
Some will do their work most effectively if they do it in a straightforward manner.
Plain sentences are as purposeful and efficient as the sentences that seem to resonate.

The way to recover your interest, your discipline, often begins on a small scale,
By fixing sentences, working on syntax,
Looking for problems in the sentences themselves.
As you work—sentence by sentence, thought by thought,
Making this phrase better, that verb stronger—your mood will lift too.
The work will rescue you instead of you rescuing it.

Now it's time to talk about the *other* reader.
Perhaps you've been wondering about her all along.
Not the reader with a genius for taking you literally,
Who always makes the wrong turn in ambiguous sentences
And stumbles over syntactical blunders,
But the other one who lives beside her in the very same brain:
Literate, curious, adaptable, intelligent, and open-minded.

Let's begin by presupposing she exists,
Which is more than your education presupposes.

Nearly everything you've been taught about writing
Assumes that the reader is plodding at best,
Always distracted and needing a surfeit of superficial cleverness
To keep his head pointed toward the text.
You'll find that assumption all around you.

We remove the unfamiliar words for him
So he'll never have the chance to learn them.
We over-reason for him, filling our prose with approximations of logic,
So he'll feel he's had a good think.

The ordinary reader—the ordinary audience—is a barren conceit.
It guarantees a shared mediocrity.

Don't preconceive the reader's limitations.
They'll become your own.

To write well, it isn't enough for you to read differently.
Imagine the reader reading differently too,
Alive to the movement of language
And the qualities of writing that depend
On an unspoken understanding between writer and
reader:
Wit, irony, inference, and implication.

Imagine a reader you can trust.

This sounds like a simple imperative.
But the difference between writing for the reader
implicit in your education
And writing for one you trust is the difference between
writing clumsily,
Using all the grappling hooks of transition and false
logic,
And writing well, able to move briskly and freely,
Going anywhere from anywhere almost instantly.

All your life you've been reading books that trusted
you,
Trusted your intelligence, your keenness,
Your ability to feel an invisible wink,
To follow any trail,
Even while you were learning in school not to trust
the reader.

. . .

The books that trusted you most may be the ones you love best.

And what happens if you trust the reader?

All the devices of distrust fall away,
The pretense of logic, the obsession with transition,
The creeping, incremental movement of sentences,
Sentences stepping on each other's heels.

With them go all the devices
Meant to overawe the reader, that aping of authority
Which even young writers learn so soon and so well—
A prose about hierarchy and its demarcations
Rather than the authority of clarity and directness.

Why would you try to overawe a reader you can trust?
The reader you can trust is a reader predisposed to trust you.
In that reciprocity lies the joy of writing and reading.
You can't trust the reader without also trusting yourself.

The trustworthy reader is alert to the way your sentences
Create promises and contracts.
These implicit promises are a descant running through your sentences.

. . .

If you write ambiguous sentences, you create a state of uncontrolled implication,
And among those implications are commitments to the reader that can't be fulfilled
Because the writer isn't aware of them.
But the reader feels them being made and broken, again and again.

Your sentences come one by one onto the stage
And leave it one by one, without assisting each other.
But they listen intently to one another,
With special attention to the promises they've made.

In the syntax and rhythm of the sentences,
In the pace of thought, the intensity of movement,
The crescendo and decrescendo,
The trustworthy reader learns the writer's habitude and how to move with it.
You converse, in a sense, with the voice on the other side of the ink.

That kind of reading is the pleasure of being summoned out of ourselves by the grace,
The ferocity, the skill of the writing before us.
How else to explain our love of even difficult writers?
Their agility evokes our agility.
We move at their speed, elliptically, obliquely,
However they move.

Imagine a cellist playing one of Bach's solo suites.
Does he consider his audience?
      (Did Bach, for that matter?)
Does he play the suite differently to audiences
Of different incomes and educations and social backgrounds?
No. The work selects its audience.

You'll be tempted to ask, "Who is the reader?"
The better question is always, "Who am I to the reader?"
And also, "How many versions of 'I' are present in this piece?"
Who said there had to be only one?

Sooner or later, you'll also wonder,
"What can I expect the reader to know?"
It's a perplexing question for writers,
A way of asking, "How much of my world overlaps with the reader's?"

Hidden behind that philosophical question is a more practical one:
"How much do I have to explain?"

It helps to remember that your prose is going to be read
Against two different backdrops:

What the reader knows about reading and what the
reader knows about life.
It's surprising how many writers forget the life part.

Trusting the reader is a way of controlling
The temptation to over-narrate, over-describe, over-
interpret, over-signify.
It lets the reader share the burden of comprehension.
This is part of the constant negotiation between writ-
ers and readers.
A good reader will follow a good writer wherever she
goes,
And the good writer will do all she can to help.

That's why learning to read your own work as a *reader,*
Not as its writer, is so helpful.
Learn to trust yourself as the reader.
You'll never know another more thoroughly.

Instead of writing for an imaginary audience of read-
ers, however large or small,
Try writing for the reader in yourself,
A stand-in for the reader you trust,
Who's always at hand and always consistent.
Like being the narrator, this is a kind of role-playing—
Impersonating the literal-minded reader and the trust-
ing reader at the same time.

.   .   .

It means trying to come to your work
Without the immense foreknowledge of having written it.
And it means imagining the reader's experience
As he gathers what he knows about your piece
Only from what each sentence reveals, one after the other.

This would be impossible if you hadn't spent so much time
As a reader yourself making your way through other writers' works,
Orienting yourself in unfamiliar worlds, sentence by sentence,
Learning characters and deciphering plots, word by word,
Absorbing arguments, and tracing the meditative currents of essays,
Undaunted by the newness of the next thing you read.

———————

Being your own reader doesn't mean you're writing only for yourself.
It isn't solipsism or egocentricity.
It's one of the writer's important economies,
A faith in the kinship between you and the reader who isn't you,
The assurance that what interests you will interest the reader

If your sentences warrant it.
This you will have to take on trust—that you and the reader
Are more alike than you like to think.
Otherwise how would any of this be possible?

Besides being your own reader, you're also your own editor.
Your only editor.
Your writing is your responsibility, first and last, in every detail.
No one will fix it or clean it up.
It's your job to be clear, precise, intelligent, resourceful, poetic, and wise
In prose of staggering clarity, all of it perfectly proofread.
That's why you became a writer, isn't it?

You're not responsible for your readers' ignorance,
And they're not responsible for your erudition.
Know what you want to know, learn what you want to learn,
Use what you want to use,
Without worrying whether you're wandering out of the reader's depth.

At the same time show a tender care
For the reader's attention, his knowledge of place and time,
His sense of his whereabouts in the pages before him.

Pause now and then to make sure he's with you.
Bring him up to the crow's nest to get a feel for the current and where you're headed.
This sounds contradictory, I know.
But then, so much of writing is.

When will you be done?
This isn't about getting to the end of the writing day and out of your head at last.
It's about knowing when a piece is finished.

This question is a variant of "How will I know when to stop revising?"
A question that rings with a certain fear,
As though you might spawn a thousand mutations of every sentence
With no means of natural selection.

"Done" isn't absolute or arbitrary.
Nor is it really about learning your limits as a writer.
It's a compromise.

This is another of the writer's economies,
Knowing how far to push a piece and when to let it go.
There's sometimes a relenting when you stop at last.
More time, more money, more research, more intelligence,
Might have made a difference.

. . .

But there's sometimes a certainty too,
The knowledge that this particular parallel universe is
now complete.

"Done enough" sounds too callow to describe the
compromise,
So call it "perfection enough,"
As perfect as possible under the circumstances.

There's no objective measure of "done."
It's an assurance within yourself,
A response to the work that's as much feeling as
judgment,
A feeling derived from your rich experience of the
completeness
Of all the books you've read in your life.

At first, "done" will come too soon.
You'll think you're finished only to find, again,
How well some sentences hide ambiguity.
Or "done" may seem too remote, an unimaginable
state of perfection
Achieved after infinite revision.

But in a certain sense, the completeness of your piece
Will have been inherent in it all along.
You come upon it with one final revision, one final fix.
It's likely to take you by surprise.

. . .

You're urging forward every word, every phrase,
Every sentence, every rhythm, until they find their
balance, their coherence.
You may think you know, at the start, what you want
that coherence to feel like.
But it won't.

So let's not talk about "done."
It's premature, something you'll discover for yourself
when the time comes.
You'll need to know two things:
You won't write a final sentence and then "The End,"
And the distance to completion will change with the
changes in the way you write.

The better question now is the more fearful one:
"How will I know when to stop revising?"
You may not be able to tell yet whether your revisions
are really improvements.

So revise toward brevity—remove words instead of
adding them.
Toward directness—language that isn't evasive or
periphrastic.
Toward simplicity—in construction and word choice.
Toward clarity—a constant lookout for ambiguity.
Toward rhythm—where it's lacking.
Toward literalness—as an antidote to obscurity.
Toward implication—the silent utterance of your
sentences.

Toward variation—always.
Toward silence—leave some.
Toward the name of the world—yours to discover.
Toward presence—the quiet authority of your prose.

And when things are really working,
That's when it's time to break what already works,
And keep breaking it
Until you find what's next.

———————————

I began this book by writing,
Know what each sentence says,
What it doesn't say,
And what it implies.

The way to keep going?
Never stop reading.
Say more than you thought you knew how to say
In sentences better than you ever imagined
For the reader who reads between the lines.

Some Prose and Some Questions

Here are some passages to experiment with as you read this book.

But let's set aside a few responses:
Whether you like a passage or not.
Whether you like the author or not.
Whether or not you think the author likes you.
Whether you like what a passage is saying.
Those aren't useful layers of response for these experiments.

Let's also set aside the question of meaning, significance.
Don't be concerned with what the author is "trying to say."
Each of these passages—with one or two possible exceptions—is bound to other passages in the work it was taken from and is therefore incomplete.

Watch yourself carefully.
You may be trying to discover things that can later be converted into meaning.
You may also find yourself trying to describe the style of the prose or its ideological or theoretical content.
Don't.
The most valuable thoughts may be the ones that

begin, "I don't know if this is important but . . ." or "This will sound like nitpicking . . .".

All you're doing is noticing what you notice.

Try to resist deciding whether what you notice is important or not.

Of course it is, even if you can't say precisely what it is you've noticed.

Begin by reading these passages aloud.

I've already listed some of the questions you might ask about these passages (on page 162).

You will think of many others.

MY BANDANNA IS ROLLED on the diagonal and retains water fairly well. I keep it knotted around my head, and now and again dip it into the river. The water is forty-six degrees. Against the temples, it is refrigerant and relieving. This has done away with the headaches that the sun caused in days before. The Arctic sun—penetrating, intense—seems not so much to shine as to strike. Even the trickles of water that run down my T-shirt feel good. Meanwhile, the river—the clearest, purest water I have ever seen flowing over rocks—breaks the light into flashes and sends them upward into the eyes. The headaches have reminded me of the kind that are sometimes caused by altitude, but, for all the fact that we have come down through mountains, we have not been higher than a few hundred feet above the level of the sea. Drifting now—a canoe, two kayaks—and thanking God it is not my turn in either of the kayaks, I lift my fish rod from the tines of a caribou rack (lashed there in mid-canoe to the duffel) and send a line flying toward a wall of bedrock by the edge of the stream. A grayling comes up and, after some hesitation, takes the lure and runs with it for a time. I disengage the lure and let the grayling go, being mindful not to wipe my hands on my shirt. Several days in use, the shirt is approaching filthy, but here among grizzly bears I would prefer to stink of humanity than of fish.

JOHN MCPHEE, *Coming into the Country*

THE DISTANCE FROM NEW ORLEANS to Alexandria is about 190 miles. The first 90 miles, from New Orleans to Baton Rouge, are on a throughway, a straight, fast road on the east side of the Mississippi, far enough back from the bank to avoid meanders, and high enough over the marshes to obviate bridges. There is nothing worth a long look. The bayous parallel the road on either side like stagnant, weed-strangled ditches, but their life is discreetly subsurface—snapping turtles, garfish, water moccasins and alligators. The mammals are water rats and muskrats and nutria, a third kind of rat. The nutria, particularly ferocious, is expropriating the other rats. Bird life, on the day we drove through, was a patrol of turkey buzzards looking down for rat cadavers. There pressed down on the landscape a smell like water that householders have inadvertently left flowers in while they went off for a summer holiday. It was an ideal setting for talk about politics.

A. J. LIEBLING, *The Earl of Louisiana*

THE TIDE WAS OUT. So far as the eye could see there stretched the matted bents of the mudflats: a soft monotony blended of grey and green and blue and purple. It had a quilted look, for the thousands of rivulets, which cast a network over it, followed the same course day in, day out, and had worn down the mud into channels between the hummocks some feet deep. To the small creatures which lived here this must have been a most fantastic landscape. At the bottom of these deep channels the tiny streams, only a few inches wide, had their established, deeply graven waterfalls, their rapids which tested to the utmost the gallantry of straws, and lakes with bays and beaches; and on the islands grass roots found purchase on the mud by gripping it and one another so that they grew into cushions of jungle, one plant rising on another like minute vegetable pagodas. The scene was incised and overstuffed with profligate ingenuity; and it was odd to think of all this elaboration being wiped out twice in every twenty-four hours, the rivulets losing their identities in the rough inundation of the tide, the springing grasses, so obstinate in their intention of making dry land out of mud, becoming the bottom of the sea. There was the same spendthrift and impermanent fabrication going on at ground level as there was over our heads, where great clouds, momentarily like castles, temples, mountains, and giant birds, were blown by the cleansing winter wind to the edges of the sky, here not clipped away by hills or streets and astonishingly far apart. There could not have been a more generous scene, nor one which was less suited to receive the remains of Mr. Setty, who from infancy had been so deeply involved in calculation, and so unhappily, who had tried keeping figures outside his head and got sent to prison for it, and had kept them inside his head and got killed for it.

REBECCA WEST, "Mr. Setty and Mr. Hume"

TO MY AUNT MAE—Mary Elizabeth Davenport Morrow (1881–1964), whose diary when I saw it after her death turned out to be a list of places, with dates, she and Uncle Buzzie (Julius Allen Morrow, 1885–1970) had visited over the years, never driving over thirty miles an hour, places like Toccoa Falls, Georgia, and

Antreville, South Carolina, as well as random sentences athwart the page, two of which face down indifference, "My father was a horse doctor, but not a common horse doctor" and "Nobody has ever loved me as much as I have loved them"—and a Mrs. Cora Shiflett, a neighbor on East Franklin Street, Anderson, South Carolina, I owe my love of reading.

GUY DAVENPORT, "On Reading"

EVEN WHEN YOU WATCH the process of coal-extraction you probably only watch it for a short time, and it is not until you begin making a few calculations that you realise what a stupendous task the "fillers" are performing. Normally each man has to clear a space four or five yards wide. The cutter has undermined the coal to the depth of five feet, so that if the seam of coal is three or four feet high, each man has to cut out, break up and load on to the belt something between seven and twelve cubic yards of coal. This is to say, taking a cubic yard as weighing twenty-seven hundredweight, that each man is shifting coal at a speed approaching two tons an hour. I have just enough experience of pick and shovel work to be able to grasp what this means. When I am digging trenches in my garden, if I shift two tons of earth during the afternoon, I feel that I have earned my tea. But earth is tractable stuff compared with coal, and I don't have to work kneeling down, a thousand feet underground, in suffocating heat and swallowing coal dust with every breath I take; nor do I have to walk a mile bent double before I begin. The miner's job would be as much beyond my power as it would be to perform on the flying trapeze or to win the Grand National. I am not a manual labourer and please God I never shall be one, but there are some kinds of manual work that I could do if I had to. At a pitch I could be a tolerable road-sweeper or an inefficient gardener or even a tenth-rate farm hand. But by no conceivable amount of effort or training could I become a coal-miner; the work would kill me in a few weeks.

GEORGE ORWELL, *The Road to Wigan Pier*

WHAT IS THE CHINESE WAR LIKE? Well, at least it isn't like wars in history books. You know, those lucid tidy maps of battles one used to study, the flanks like neat little cubes, the pincer movements working with mathematical precision, the reinforcements never failing to arrive. War isn't like that. War is bombing an already disused arsenal, missing it and killing a few old women. War is lying in a stable with a gangrenous leg. War is drinking hot water in a barn and worrying about one's wife. War is a handful of lost and terrified men in the mountains, shooting at something moving in the undergrowth. War is waiting for days with nothing to do, shouting down a dead telephone, going without sleep and sex and a wash. War is untidy, inefficient, obscene, and largely a matter of chance.

W. H. AUDEN, 1939

THE WINTER FIRES OF NEW YORK burn everywhere like the ghats in Benares. On the valueless land north of the ship canal some children, dressed like aviators, are burning a Christmas tree. An ashcan is blazing on the banks of the river. Rubbish fires glow in the backyards of Harlem. Farther south, where a slum is being cleared, there is a large conflagration of old lathes. Another rubbish barrel and another Christmas tree are burning on Ninety-sixth Street. On the curb at Eighty-third Street an old wicker table is being consumed with fire. In a vacant lot in the fifties some children are burning a mattress. South of the United Nations there is a big fire of cardboard cartons behind a grocery store. Many fires burn in the gutters and backyards of the slums; there are bonfires of wooden crates in front of the fish market and on Battery Park, untended, an iron basket, full of waste, lights the gloom as all these other fires do on a winter dusk when the dark begins to fall before the lights go on.

JOHN CHEEVER, *Journals*

IN THE SUMMER OF 1943 I was eight, and my father and mother and small brother and I were at Peterson Field in Colorado Springs. A hot wind blew through that summer, blew until it seemed that before August broke, all the dust in Kansas would be in Colorado, would have drifted over the tar-paper barracks and the temporary strip and stopped only when it hit Pikes Peak. There was not much to do, a summer like that: there was the day they brought in the first B-29, an event to remember but scarcely a vacation program. There was an Officers' Club, but no swimming pool; all the Officers' Club had of interest was artificial blue rain behind the bar. The rain interested me a good deal, but I could not spend the summer watching it, and so we went, my brother and I, to the movies.

We went three and four afternoons a week, sat on folding chairs in the darkened Quonset hut which served as a theater, and it was there, that summer of 1943 while the hot wind blew outside, that I first saw John Wayne. Saw the walk, heard the voice. Heard him tell the girl in a picture called *War of the Wildcats* that he would build her a house, "at the bend in the river where the cottonwoods grow."

As it happened I did not grow up to be the kind of woman who is the heroine in a Western, and although the men I have known have had many virtues and have taken me to live in many places I have come to love, they have never been John Wayne, and they have never taken me to that bend in the river where the cottonwoods grow. Deep in that part of my heart where the artificial rain forever falls, that is still the line I wait to hear.

JOAN DIDION, "John Wayne: A Love Song,"
in *Slouching Towards Bethlehem*

I GREW UP IN THE MIDWEST and despised horses. The ones I rode struck me as stupid and untrustworthy. I went to Wyoming when I was young, and the ones there were worse. On a cold morning, two out of three would buck you down. They were, I felt, an ugly necessity for where a truck wouldn't go.

I've been kicked, stepped on, and bitten. Bitten I liked least. My most trustworthy saddle horse leaned over once while I was cinching him up and clamped on my upper leg, turning the thigh into what looked like a Central American sunset. I threw him down on the ground, half-hitched his feet together, and put a tarp over him. I let him up two hours later: he thought I was the greatest man in the world, one he wouldn't think of biting. Horses only remember the end of the story.

TOM MCGUANE, "Roping, from A to B,"
in *An Outside Chance*

THIS MORNING, an invasion of tiny black ants. One by one they appear, out of nowhere—that's their charm too!—moving single file across the white Parsons table where I am sitting, trying without much success to write a poem. A poem of only three or four lines is what I want, something short, tight, mean, I want it to hurt like a white-hot wire up the nostrils, small and compact and turned in upon itself with the density of a hunk of rock from Jupiter . . .

But here come the ants: harbingers, you might say, of spring. One by one they appear on the dazzling white table and one by one I kill them with a forefinger, my deft right forefinger, mashing each against the surface of the table and dropping it into a wastebasket at my side. Idle labor, mesmerizing, effortless, and I'm curious as to how long I can do it, sit here in the brilliant March sunshine killing ants with my right forefinger, how long I, and the ants, can keep it up.

After a while I realize that I can do it a long time. And that I've written my poem.

JOYCE CAROL OATES, "Against Nature"

I CARE NOT TO BE CARRIED with the tide, that smoothly bears human life to eternity; and reluct at the inevitable course of destiny. I am in love with this green earth; the face of town and country; the unspeakable rural solitudes, and the sweet security of streets. I would set up my tabernacle here. I am content to stand still at the age to which I am arrived; I, and my friends: to be no younger, no richer, no handsomer. I do not want to be weaned by age; or drop, like mellow fruit, as they say, into the grave. Any alteration, on this earth of mine, in diet or in lodging, puzzles and discomposes me. My household-gods plant a terrible fixed foot, and are not rooted up without blood. They do not willingly seek Lavinian shores. A new state of being staggers me.

Sun, and sky, and breeze, and solitary walks, and summer holidays, and the greenness of fields, and the delicious juices of meats and fishes, and society, and the cheerful glass, and candle-light, and fire-side conversations, and innocent vanities, and jests, and *irony itself*—do these things go out with life?

CHARLES LAMB, "New Year's Eve," 1821

Consider each sentence on its own, disconnected from the whole.

(That's inevitably one of the ways you consider the sentences *you* make.)

Pay attention to the ordinary way you might say something.

Think of that as the backdrop for the questions you ask these sentences.

. . .

See anything peculiar?

A phrasing you didn't expect?

A rhythm more pronounced than its surroundings?

A word in a position that sounds odd?

Note in each passage how variant in structure the sentences are—no two quite the same in shape.

And how, when they're invariant, you can feel the reason why. (See Auden.)

How closely—or how loosely—are the sentences in a passage bound to each other?

Can you feel a gap between them—something indiscernible going unsaid?

Are there sentences that explain or fulfill the sentence that precedes them?

That build a rhythm with other sentences?

Sentences that misdirect or decoy the reader?

A sentence that's working harder than the others—doing more to draw or turn the reader's attention?

Let yourself ask the question why.

Why is the author choosing this word, writing that sentence that way?

Don't expect to find *an* answer.

Expect to find some possibilities.

Here are some examples.

Why does John McPhee use the word "refrigerant"?

Why not simply "cooling"?

And why "the temples" and not "my temples"?

And why "days before," as if this were legend, or "level of the sea" instead of "sea level"?

Notice the word "there" in the parenthetical phrase near the end of the passage.

Can you feel how it orients us? How it situates McPhee?

————————

Take a look at the verbs (and the sentence structures) in the passage by A. J. Liebling.

For the most part, they're pretty plain: "is," "are," "was."

So where does the life of this passage come from?

Repetition does one kind of work here, another, vastly different kind in the passage by Auden.

Consider the economy of using the verb "to obviate."

Can you see that Liebling has left the vase out of the penultimate sentence?

And how much it would complicate things to include it?

————————

Slow down a great deal as you read the passage by Rebecca West.

If necessary, take a pen or pencil and indicate the

breaks between phrases or clauses where she hasn't already used a mark of punctuation.

Then read it aloud again.

In this passage, it would be useful to sort through the nouns and see what kinds there are, what categories they fall into.

It would also be useful to break this into a series of short sentences—as short as possible ("The tide was out")—and then watch how West recombines them into the texture, the rhythm, of her prose.

Look for the modifiers in this passage—individual words but also, more important, entire phrases.

Pay attention to the way they extend and structure West's sentences.

———

In Guy Davenport, too, it's worth seeing if you can find the separate assertions that underlie this extraordinary single sentence and turn them into their own sentences:

Over the years, she and Uncle Buzzie had visited places like Toccoa Falls, Georgia, and Antreville, South Carolina. They never drove faster than thirty miles an hour.

Then look at the words that are left behind.

This is a sentence built by suspension—a sense of equivalence—not subordination. How does that come about?

And *why* would Davenport write a sentence like this?

In George Orwell, what's the difference between the sentence he gives us, "When I am digging trenches in my garden, if I shift two tons of earth during the afternoon, I feel that I have earned my tea," and *If I shift two tons of earth during the afternoon when I am digging trenches in my garden, I feel that I have earned my tea*?

There's nothing elaborate or uncommon about the words that appear in any of these sentences.

But notice how patient he is as he builds this passage, step-by-step, rising from calculation to astonishment to a kind of self-abnegation.

And yet can you feel the lack of thus-ness—the way these sentences stand side by side, each one on its own feet?

How tempting it would have been to supply this paragraph with logical indicators to bind the sentences together.

This passage by W. H. Auden was written as a radio talk for the BBC—to be read aloud, or rather spoken into a microphone.

And yet apart from "Well, at least" and "You know"—which suggest an intimate, colloquial connection with his audience—there's nothing here that doesn't sound written to be read silently.

The sentences that begin "War is . . ." look repetitive, but it's worth noting how un-repetitive they really are, structurally and rhythmically.

Listen, too, for the restraint in this passage, the things Auden refrains from doing.

For instance: he avoids the temptation to build a crescendo into the sentences beginning "War is . . ."

He also doesn't let these sentences become more parallel than they need to be.

Though everything is just as he wants it in this paragraph, it doesn't feel overdetermined.

He's paying more attention to what the reader hears than he is to the possibility of building more pattern into his prose.

—————

The passage from John Cheever's *Journals*—what kinds of journals are these?

Clearly not the kind we often mean: daily jottings, notes on life and living, an informal archive of emotions and events.

At play here is perception—the gathering in his mind of all these fires—but also the play of sentence making: How many ways are there to say something is burning?

This passage has no larger purpose than to exist, to work out, for a moment, the possibilities of some sentences.

And yet we feel its inadvertent testimony—the

vision of a city lit up by small conflagrations, a city where children instinctively gather near the flames.

Those children dressed like aviators persist.

Look carefully at the rhythm of the last sentence, how it keeps wanting to settle into a familiar, steady beat and how Cheever keeps it from doing so.

And if you lose your sense of what rhythm is, simply remember the line Joan Didion quotes in this passage: "at the bend in the river where the cottonwoods grow."

But look for the counter-rhythms, the passages that are more abrupt, less sinuous.

Where do those staccato pulses come from?

This is also a passage to help you remember how brief—and how extensive—rhythm can be.

The first paragraph is neutral, almost plain, except when Didion turns to the hot wind and the dust—an extended rhythm.

And also the very end: "and so we went, my brother and I, to the movies"—a brief rhythmic pulse to close the paragraph and open what follows.

Remove the word "forever" from the last sentence.

The first time you read the sentence that way, it seems to stumble over itself.

But can you read it without "forever" and still find the rhythm of its opening clause?

Now reinsert "forever."

This is a test you need to be performing on your own sentences.

In the passage from Tom McGuane, think about the sentence "Bitten I liked least."

A "correct" way to say this might be: *I liked being bitten least.*

But there's a moment of discovery in the gap between "I've been kicked, stepped on, and bitten. Bitten I liked least"—a chance to intensify the compression, the terseness, you can feel all through this passage.

Also a chance, in that bitten-off sentence, to intensify the reader's sense of the writer's character.

The essay containing this passage by Joyce Carol Oates also contains the epigraph I borrow from her.

The ellipsis at the end of the first paragraph is hers.

I'll let you find the questions and discover the experiments to perform here.

We've been taught to create a kind of vocal uniformity in our prose—one voice, one tone, a very narrow band of ourselves visible to the reader.

Charles Lamb defies all this, gloriously.

There is something luminescent and completely various in the versions of himself he presents in this essay—as though each emotion revealed a different Lamb.

Don't worry about "Lavinian."

But do pause to admire his use of the verb "reluct"— the root of the only form we use, "reluctance."

And just as Lamb is the most various of all these authors, in the character he presents the reader, this is also the most various passage rhythmically and in the shape of its sentences.

How hard now to say, simply, "I am in love with this green earth."

Some Practical Problems

Reading these sentences—and my commentary on them—you'll be tempted to side with the writer, to think, "I know what he means" or "I can see what she's saying." But that's because it feels so normal to try to deduce the meaning of the sentence instead of observing what its words actually say. We're so trained to read for meaning—to look through the sentence to what we think is the author's intention—that in our search for it we're prepared to disregard the literal significance of the prose itself.

You may also be tempted to say, "Maybe the writer wants it that way." But you can only judge intentionality in context. If all the sentences in a piece are clear and sharp, then perhaps—perhaps!—we can say that a slightly aberrant sentence is intentional, if there seems to be a reason for it. But if many of the sentences in a piece are unclear, ambiguous, or weak, we have to assume that intention is irrelevant—indiscernible at best. We have to assume the writer lacks control.

These sentences were written by excellent college students who went on to be very good writers. They— the sentences, that is—are no worse and no better than the sentences you'll come across on any day, in any medium, anywhere.

———————

She didn't trust him with his accent or his gentle demeanor.

Note how "with" distorts the sentence. It could read, *She didn't trust him.* Or *She didn't trust his accent or his gentle demeanor.* And note too that "trust him with" is an active, meaningful locution in English, for example, *She didn't want to trust him with her new car.* You can feel the pressure of that locution in this sentence, even though it doesn't belong there.

———————

I despise the feeling of something falling apart in your body.

Note the shift from the first to the second person.

This makes no sense unless the author is despising you. The second person requires some attention, or it easily goes awry.

———————

Erica wobbled uncertainly as she tried to sit down on the stool next to me.

Can one wobble *certainly*? "Uncertainly" is implicit in "wobble" and "tried." An example of the kind of redundancy that adverbs often create.

———————

The buffet of diseases, cancers, viruses, and overall deteriorations our present world has to offer is impressive and wary.

Several problems, beginning with an unworkable metaphor: the "wary buffet." The adjectives at the end of the sentence must modify the subject. The author of this sentence has completely lost track of the beginning by the time he reaches the end.

———————

By the time I was 11 the milieu of doubts, questions, and skepticism had culminated into a daunting tangle of despondent confusion.

The trouble? Words used incorrectly: "milieu" and "culminated." By "milieu," he means something like "mix" or "combination." No such thing as "culminating into"—"culminating in" is possible. This would be a tolerable sentence if it said, *By the time I was eleven, my doubts, questions, and skepticism had turned into despondent confusion.* Note the metaphorical feeling of "tangle"—it wants to be more literal, and plural, than "despondent confusion" allows. A tangle of feelings, yes. A tangle of confusion, no.

Her hair, dyed black, is neatly quaffed.

A delightful sentence if the author means that her hair is easily imbibed. The word is "coiffed." This problem is solved by using the dictionary.

Grimy rinds of snow still squat along the northern walls of buildings.

"Grimy rinds of snow" is good. But look what the word "squat" does. It animates the already metaphorical "rinds." In regular life, rinds don't squat.

This is a room where mornings are had in loneliness, and evenings are had in relief.

A nice attempt flawed by a very weak verb—"are had." Slight additional confusion because, as a locution, "to be had" has a very different meaning, as in "We were had." And why the weak verb? The effort to heighten the parallel between mornings and evenings. But could the sentence be as powerful without a parallel structure? Certainly. Shanghaied by a syntactical choice.

_____

His gaze was fixed to the ground with an occasional glance at the horizon for a brief inspection of the distance to the next knoll.

He gazed at the ground, but sometimes he glanced at the horizon. Note how "was fixed" throws everything into disarray. There's a kind of verbal poverty in this sentence. Why only one verb? And a flawed one at that? Note how "with an occasional glance" and "for a brief inspection" are trying to do the work of verbs. But they can't. "To glance" and "to inspect" have been turned into nouns, which depletes their energy. Note too that "gaze" is the origin of much of this trouble. The verb again gets turned into a noun, and a noun that's incapable of action. "He," as the subject, offers better verb choices than "his gaze."

_____

The lifejacket dug into my armpits as heavy boots pulled my legs down.

"As" is nearly always trouble. What's it doing here?

Insisting on simultaneity? "And" would work as well and more simply. Note the feeling that these could be someone else's—anyone else's—boots. And note too the feeling that the legs are going down without the rest of this writer's body.

On occasion Etta James may faintly be heard singing in the kitchen, a creek throughout the floorboards or whining from the attic ceiling.

Etta James seems to be whining from the attic ceiling and also to have become, somehow, a stream flowing through the house. Chaos. Instead of "On occasion" try "sometimes." "Creek" does not equal "creak." From the attic—not from the attic ceiling, which is the ceiling *over* the attic, not over the room below the attic. This attempt to list some of the sounds in a house goes completely awry—and why? Because one verb—"may faintly be heard"—is trying to govern "creak" and "whining." And why? Because the sentence is fundamentally passive. *You can hear Etta James singing faintly in the kitchen. You can also hear creaking in the floorboards and a whining from the attic.* And what if we revise further and remove the verbs of perception? *Sometimes Etta James sings faintly from the kitchen. The floorboards creak, and the ceiling whines.*

So I have found myself inside this intensely feminine world in much the same way as the crossing-dressing men in *Some Like It Hot* when they infiltrate an all-woman jazz band.

A typo makes it sound as though the author means these men dress up as street crossings. What's the trouble here? The men in *Some Like It Hot* (and the actors who play them) have names, but the author doesn't know them, or won't use them if he does. He isn't sure whether he can count on the reader's knowing the movie. If he was sure, he wouldn't have added "when they infiltrate an all-woman jazz band." Also, "much like the cross-dressing men" is better than "in much the same way as the cross-dressing men" simply because it uses fewer words. Even better is "much like Tony Curtis and Jack Lemmon."

In the last row, I sat between my mother and father, the latter of whom was to die three months later.

"In the last row" sounds oddly placed, though that depends on context. Note that "the latter of whom" over-specifies—and over-formalizes—a much simpler construction: *I sat between my mother and father, who was to die three months later.* Notice that there's no confusion about who will be dying, even without "the latter of whom." That phrase and the forward-looking past tense verb—"was to die"—do a very good job of draining any emotion out of this sentence. Also, there's an odd sense of intentionality in "was to die." What's wrong with this version: *I sat between my mother and father, who died three months later*? It's ambiguous. Do they both die? Its ambiguity can be resolved easily enough: *I sat between my mother and my father, who died three months later.*

Throughout the year, the chubby pigeons would perch on the south-facing roof of her home.

This sentence implies that svelte pigeons perched elsewhere. Removing "the" from "the chubby pigeons" helps. As does turning "would perch" into "perched." The habitual nature of their perching—which is what "would perch" is meant to suggest—has already been established by "throughout the year."

Since I was little, Wallace has been around.

Notice how different this version of the sentence sounds: *Wallace has been around since I was little.* What's the difference? "Since." In the original, it has the ambiguous overtone of "because," which vanishes in the revision.

He shines from stem to stern due to his three chunky gold rings and spiffy dress shoes.

Perhaps, if he's wearing chunky gold rings on his stem and spiffy dress shoes on his stern. But I doubt he is. Betrayed by a cliché. "Due to" does the work a verb should be doing.

———

A lot of the older campers still look to me as someone they can confide in.

A syntactical trap. The sentence starts out reading as though it might say something like, "A lot of the older campers still look to me like children." Saying "still regard me" would help. But what if the sentence simply said, *A lot of the older campers still confide in me*?

———

There is an old man who lives there.

How did this sentence escape fixing? Because it became invisible, that's how. *An old man lives there.*

———

When the Germans sensed the end of the war, they stopped actively murdering the newborn babies in the camp.

This has the unfortunate effect of implying that "passively murdering" is possible.

———————

All of them are in some kind of ill-fitting jacket.

Of course it's an ill-fitting jacket. All of them are in it. Plural persons in a singular jacket.

———————

The family photos on my mother's side are scarce.

Look at what the word "the" does. It posits the existence of family photos which are then scarce, as if they'd run away from home. Remove "the" and the sentence makes much more sense.

———————

Diane's death must have shocked the family into the realization that in the end death would come for them all.

"Realizing that death," not "the realization that in the end death." Replace the noun phrase with a verb form.

———————

Children in this age group are generally developing social awareness skills where they become aware of the role of the self in relation to others.

"Where" is trying vainly to serve as a relative pronoun, which it's not. All it really succeeds in doing is holding a redundancy apart. *Children in this age-group are generally just becoming aware of the role of the self in relation to others.*

Denizens of America's northwest corner are not exceptionally fond of products derived from the flesh of swine, of course; however they, like any Americans, were keen to be the beneficiaries of the excessive political patronage known as "pork barrel legislation."

This is an attempt at humor by being orotund. Is it really true that people in Washington and Oregon don't like bacon? After the semicolon, the pork becomes metaphorical. This sentence is studded with the attributes of prose as it is usually taught today. It's periphrastic, illogical while insisting on its logic, and awkwardly metaphorical, and the author is buried somewhere under the rubble.

I studied abroad the fall of my junior year in France.

Betrayed by two words that like to stick together: "study abroad." *I studied in France the fall of my junior year.* The abroadness will be implicit, unless this sentence was written in France.

I am not a typical daughter of Seattle, though I do love the Mariners with a passion that can cause the uninitiated ballpark companion to flee Safeco Field for fear of losing an eardrum.

The last half of the sentence can be paraphrased thus: *I scream so loud it hurts my friend's ear.* Nothing is gained by loosing this avalanche of words.

As I dive in, the water gives me its usual jolt in the stomach, but I welcome the shock and hang for a moment in the closest approximation of flight I know.

Note how time runs backward and then stops in this sentence. First the diver feels the jolt of the water but welcomes the shock even in mid-dive, before he has hit the water.

The two families line up like competing rugby teams. The bride takes the place of the rugby ball standing between the two groups in full wedding regalia.

A metaphor that begins to work and then fails completely. The bride as rugby ball is deeply unfortunate.

Whatever ghosts were left in Pompeii had long disappeared, leaving behind twisted plaster casts and British families on holiday.

There's a nice idea behind this sentence, but "leaving behind" must modify "ghosts," which makes them sound as though they'd littered the site with British families on holiday.

Exempt from army duty until the close of the war because of a lame leg it was noticed at the shooting range that he was a good shot and he was told that someone like him could be useful at the front.

Automatic revision: make this two sentences, probably three. Note that "it" was exempt from army duty. And "it" has a lame leg. The difficulty? The passive voice—"it was noticed . . . that" and "he was told that"—governs the sentence. Any sentence containing "it was noticed that" qualifies for instant demolition and reconstruction. Everything about this sentence— "army duty," "the close of the war," "someone like him could be useful"—is fuzzy.

One at a time I pull my feet up to my knees and wipe my legs dry.

Written by a contortionist. With telescoping legs, it sounds like.

In front of you a grassy meadow dusted with colorful flora extends.

Translated from the German. This sentence is trying to be expressive, descriptive. But "dusted"? "Colorful flora" hides the names of all the wildflowers in that meadow—names that could be looked up and used. This sentence is trying hard not to say, *There's a grassy meadow.* But why? At least that doesn't sound like a peculiar inversion of ordinary syntax.

Throughout the trip we had tried, despite our cameras and the other tourists, to pretend that we were true Parisians. We ordered in broken sentences and struck up awkward conversations with anyone willing to put up with us.

Note that the second sentence is implicitly going to tell us what true Parisians are like. Not like we thought.

About halfway through, I saw to my utmost horror that I could not apply a particular symbol to what I was typing.

Why be hyperbolic here? Hang on to your utmost horror. You may need it for something genuinely horrifying. "Apply a particular symbol to what I was typing"? I think the writer means he didn't know the keystroke for the symbol he wanted to use. Writers often try to be humorous by being hyperbolic. They never succeed.

———————

There are at least eight places to eat crappy food within eyesight from where you stand.

"From where you stand" is unnecessary. Just plain "nearby" would be a welcome substitute for "within eyesight from where you stand."

———————

Those walking on solid ground might lose their hats in a gust of wind, but the manic depressive stands on a seasonal tightrope.

Notice that "but" is being asked to do what it can't possibly do: yoke together these two clauses. We have no idea what contradiction might exist here, if only because the first clause sounds literally plausible while the second is metaphorically confusing. "A seasonal tightrope"?

———————

Occasional cars flash past us.

"Occasional" modifies "cars." That's the problem. How can a car be occasional? This use turns an adverb into an adjective. "Occasional," like "random" and "typical" and even "stereotypical," is often—or even occasionally—used in an almost meaningless way. Don't make time or frequency an attribute of the vehicle. Let the time or frequency indicator stand on its own. *Cars flash past us now and then.*

In a steep inner gorge, a sandstone amphitheatre has formed with a ribbon waterfall cascading from its hundred-foot precipice.

What's the problem? "With." It's trying to be both conjunction and relative pronoun when all it can be is a plain preposition. It also obscures the motion of the ribbon waterfall which "cascades" from a (not "its") hundred-foot precipice.

Displayed in glass cases and lit up like jewelry, tuna is cherished in Japan.

If the tuna comes first, the sentence won't sound so strange. *Tuna is cherished in Japan, even displayed in glass cases and lit up like jewelry.*

An array of noble mountains surround the valley. Robust with pines, spruces, and aspens, they are colorfully vibrant in the warm months.

Can you feel the emptiness of the modifiers here— "noble," "robust," "colorfully vibrant"? And note that summarizing word, "array." *Mountains surround the valley.*

My dad and I are similar in that we both hate "stuff."

"Are similar in that we" equals "both." *My dad and I both hate "stuff."* Note that you can even do without "both."

He hunched his shoulders, placed one arm on his left leg, and slid into the passenger seat before reaching across his body for his seatbelt.

Can you actually visualize this action? No. Descriptions of physical action require incredible care because we read them with our bodies as well as our brains.

With those closest to me, I don't think twice about taking an unsolicited bite, whereas with newer acquaintances, I worry my probing fork will injure a tenuous relationship.

This writer is having trouble managing her stilts. *I don't worry about stealing a bite from friends. But I do if it's a new acquaintance.* "Whereas," "unsolicited," "tenuous relationship"—all trouble, as is the fact that the literal fork implicit in the first half of the sentence suddenly performs a metaphorical action in the second half.

———————

We hold a mythological view of soldiers. We see them fly off filled with ideology and return wearied and homesick.

Note how the first sentence leads us to expect an explanation in the second sentence—an explanation of what the "mythological view" is. But it isn't forthcoming. And note too the ambiguity in the second sentence. It sounds very much as though we see the soldiers off and then return home ourselves feeling wearied and homesick. Filled with ideology?

———————

Lovers on blankets support the theory that Sevillanos are more public with their affection than lovers anywhere else in the world.

But lovers without blankets disagree. The writer

needs to return to the fundamental question: What am I trying to say? Losing "theory" would be a good place to start.

The small tube of sunblock weighs little in my right hand.

But it's much heavier when I hold it in my left. This sentence seems to be trying to say, *I'm holding a small tube of sunblock in my right hand.*

The watching of Super Bowl commercials has truly become a sacred tradition in this country.

"Watching," not "the watching of"—verb form versus noun phrase. This sentence dies by overemphasis. Get rid of "truly" and "sacred." In other words, let the sentence relax and trust that the reader will take your point. You don't have to be so insistent.

Even with my drapes pulled back, there's not much visibility from where I sit.

The possessive pronoun goes awry. This writer seems to be wearing curtains instead of eyeglasses.

"The drapes." And how about *I can't see much from where I sit*? "There's not much visibility" could mean there's a heavy ground fog in the room. That's how the word "visibility" is used outside the peculiar world of this sentence.

————————

The architecture was gray and beautiful and old and stretched out in all directions.

No, the buildings—but never the architecture.

————————

The woman is twenty-eight, with the leathery sun-worn skin of a retired couple from Florida.

What a strange woman this is, to have the skin of a retired Florida couple in her possession. How could her sun-worn skin (nice phrase) resemble that of a couple? Why is she being compared to two people? It must have been some couple to have only one skin.

————————

My mother had started planning this pilgrimage since the day I was born.

"Since"? And why the compound past? *My mother started planning this pilgrimage the day I was born.* Or *My mother has been planning this pilgrimage since the day I was born.* The continuity of "since" requires the continuity of "has been planning."

She looked straight at me as she pulled the steering wheel around to make a graceful turn as she shook her head and said: "What a waste; I just don't get it."

"As" runs amok. Breaking this into at least two sentences would help eliminate "as."

The Lincoln-Marti School resides in Little Havana, Miami.

"Resides"? The author is clearly trying not to use "is." But why? It's simple and economical and doesn't make the reader feel as though the Lincoln-Marti School had retired to Florida.

Bread, rice, and bananas constituted my diet.

Ugly in so many ways. Why not choose a subject that is capable of eating? *I ate mostly bread, rice, and bananas.* "Constituted" is the kind of verb—abstract, dull, essentially passive, academic—that should immediately send you hunting for a stronger, more active one.

I had never seen the word "hubris" and allowed my familiarity with the similarly concluded word "debris" to guide my pronunciation.

Can you hear the writer's distrust of the reader (or of herself), as though we might not notice that "hubris" and "debris" both end in "ris"? *I'd never seen the word "hubris," so I pronounced it like "debris."*

I recall listening to a ten-minute soliloquy concerning the tomatoes in the refrigerator, which then moved from item to item on the shelves and kitchen table.

Can you feel the tomatoes moving about in this sentence? "Which" wants to point to "soliloquy" but can't.

The small houses are considered "quaint," with their well-manicured lawns and expensive landscaping of topiary, hedges, well-pruned fruit trees, cobbled footpaths lined with decorative pathlights.

Look what "with" does. It allows the writer to jumble together a pile of nouns and adjectives without going to the bother of constructing a sentence using verbs. Notice how "with" replaces syntactical possibilities that would make this a much stronger sentence.

If there is one landmark here, it is not the 335,024-square-foot anchor store so big it takes up two buildings.

After the opening phrase, we expect to learn what the one landmark is, not what it is not. A promise to the reader is not fulfilled.

While hospitals charge hundreds of thousands of rupees for a prosthetic leg, Jaipur Foot charges two thousand.

The first word is doing the steering, as if readers won't grasp the internal logic of the sentence unless we get a good long glimpse of it coming. *Hospitals charge hundreds of thousands of rupees for a prosthetic leg. Jaipur Foot charges two thousand.* The contrast is perfectly clear even without pointing to it.

Then the whole cat rises and stretches, arching its back and driving each leg into the ground until it quivers.

Pronoun problems. The antecedent of "it" is clearly meant to be "leg," and yet technically it is "ground"—the noun closest to the pronoun. This cat makes the ground quiver.

After seven hours of zooming, dropping, soaring and twisting through the air, the day had come to its natural end.

The day loves to zoom, drop, soar, and twist through the air. The opening phrase *must* modify the subject of the sentence. But it doesn't.

Los Angeles is the largest city in California with a population of over 4,997,340 spanning 498 square miles.

What does this sentence actually say? That of all the cities in California with a population of over 4,997,340 spanning 498 square miles, Los Angeles is the largest, somehow. Again, the word "with" is the culprit. A comma after California would help, but the sentence would still be weak syntactically. "With" is not remotely strong enough to sustain a sentence like this.

Every morning, just before 9 a.m., artists begin to funnel into the building, as one by one, with deliberate steps, they get off the Paratransit bus.

The artists somehow funnel into the building while at the same time getting off the Paratransit bus. The problem? The overall sequence of the sentence, certainly. How about getting them off the bus first and then having them funnel into the building? But the problem is also "as," which insists on simultaneity. Note that reality is simply imperceptible in this sentence.

A world away from his son and his granddaughters, after over a year of suffering of Alzheimer's and diabetes, he died alone in a hospital in Taiwan.

A simple, effective revision—put the right phrase in the right place. *After months of suffering from Alzheimer's and diabetes, he died alone in a hospital in Taiwan, a world away from his son and granddaughters.*

Her clothes were nondescript, a white t-shirt and jean shorts.

And yet the writer can describe them. How about *She wore a white T-shirt and jean shorts*? The nature of her clothing—its plainness, its simplicity, even its nondescriptness—will be apparent to the reader.

Under the bridges connecting the canals' sides, there are shacks built from scrap metal and wood.

As if the bridges had a function other than connecting the sides of the canals. *Under the bridges are shacks built from scrap metal and wood.*

What we do share in common, though, is our voice.

"Share" implies "in common." And note how the force of the word "though" is already implicit in the very structure of the first four words—"what we do share." *What we do share is our voice.*

As you enter town, you're guided down Main Street by two Quaker burial grounds, one on either side of the road.

These Quaker burial grounds sound rather like traffic cops. The only way to fix this sentence is to back out of it entirely. Instead of writing from the perspective of a procession into town, describe the town and then let someone (if necessary) proceed into it.

In the distance, elephants and buffalo lumber across ancestral stomping grounds.

We say, "These are my old stomping grounds," without implying that we actually stomped there. And yet somehow, in this sentence, it's hard to avoid the picture of elephants and buffalo stomping on their ancestral grounds. What the writer is trying to say has been distorted by the unbidden presence of a cliché.

––––––––––

There are constantly trucks flowing in and out of National Meats.

The natural subject of this sentence is "trucks." *Trucks flow in and out of National Meats.* But trucks are bad at flowing. Perhaps "A stream of trucks flows . . ." But perhaps "flow" is a bigger problem than it's worth.

––––––––––

It was on a heated summer day when my partner Heather and I were assigned to patrol Riverside County.

"Heated"? This makes the day sound as though it had been warmed artificially or was perhaps angry with someone. And note how cumbersome the overall structure of the sentence is—largely because it begins with "It was on a . . ." *On a hot summer day, my partner Heather and I were assigned to patrol Riverside County.* This is less emphatic than the writer's version, but then the writer's version is also clumsy, and we can't tell what's really being emphasized or set up.

––––––––––

Following the fence we built the day before, we had come across a mud wallow, the calling card of wild pigs and a sore in ranchers' sides.

The pasts are confused. "Had built" and "came." Asking a wallow to be a pig calling card and a rancher's sore at the same time is asking too much.

By 1556, biographer Giorgio Vasari had written that *The Last Supper* was ruined.

This sounds like an assertion about Vasari rather than an assertion about *The Last Supper*. What the sentence is trying to say is this: as early as 1556, some people thought *The Last Supper* was already ruined. This sentence is telling us something different. It could be saying, for instance, that at last, by 1556, the notoriously slow-writing Giorgio Vasari was able to write that *The Last Supper* was ruined. Also, note how inadequate that defining epithet—"biographer"—is. This is a journalistic habit, and a bad one.

We knew our miserable one mile per hour trekking rate was decreasing exponentially as we pressed on.

This sentence sounds neatly scientific, doesn't it? And yet it indulges in false specificity. If their rate of progress really did decrease exponentially, they'd never get there. Note how the action of walking—which should elicit a verb—vanishes from this sentence, thanks to "our miserable one mile per hour trekking rate."

I leaned against the parapet as the wind blasted me and looked out over the sea.

The wind likes to look out over the sea whenever it can. Who doesn't? Note how useless "as" is here.

She's wearing tapered, elastic-waist jeans that hang 2 inches above her ankles, and an oversized white sweatshirt with a blobby pink heart in the center.

How low is she wearing her jeans? We have to be able to picture how she actually wears them. At the very least, the sentence shouldn't actively prevent us from picturing it, the way this one does.

Kaneisha desperately wanted me to buy new clothes because mine were so bad that they embarrass everyone in their proximity.

Notice how the author suddenly seems to have vanished from her clothing. *Kaneisha desperately wanted me to buy new clothes because mine were so embarrassing.*

It is especially nice to sit there in the evening, when the sun has just set or is in the process of setting.

Or is only a few minutes away from beginning the process of setting or perhaps even beginning the process of just having finished setting. Simplify: when the sun is setting. That's enough.

My hometown gets less annual rainfall than Atlanta or Boston, but somehow we've acquired the gray reputation. Fine by me—our bad rap keeps too many Californians from moving north.

Note how the end of the second sentence completely contradicts the writer's meaning. It says, literally, that she wishes more Californians would move north. Get rid of "too many" and the sentence begins to say something sensible.

But perhaps living in Nevada would enable me an appreciation of beauty in scarcity.

"An appreciation of"? A noun phrase. No energy. Static. "To appreciate"? A verb. Better, but not perfect. Never substitute noun phrases for verbs. "Enable me"? How about this: *But perhaps living in Nevada would teach me to see the beauty in scarcity?*

The waves are loud as they crash against the beach.

Remove "as." Assume that "crash" contains the quality of loudness. *The waves crash against the beach.*

It is a comforting smell, evoking Proustian memories of sledding and snow and knitted mittens.

Yes, we now associate all sensory memory with Marcel Proust. We just didn't know he spent so much time sledding in his knitted mittens.

The world is calm, quiet, indifferent, moving at its own pace unfettered by the frenzy of human activity.

The writer has no idea what "fetter" means, much less "unfettered."

Capitola is outside the picture window.

It would be alarming if Capitola was *inside* the picture window. Even the slightest effort will produce a more useful, descriptive sentence.

The week before my flight home departed, we decided to explore drugs.

How about "the week before I flew home"? That yields a verb instead of a noun and removes the unnecessary "departed." And the phrase "explore drugs"? Strictly a billboard cliché. No one would ever say, "Let's explore drugs," except ironically. No trace of irony here.

———————

The view from the small balcony was of other apartment buildings.

What tells you that this sentence needs revising? How about the appalling "was of"? Can you feel how this sentence was written? Beginning with "the view" seemed to make sense. But note how summarizing that word is and how it excludes the presence of anyone capable of doing the viewing.

———————

I have never found words, never heard or read any, that would have alleviated the aching and emptiness I always felt following death.

This sentence was written by someone who has died many times. Also "would have" is unnecessary. *I have never found words that ease the aching and emptiness I feel.* Make the dying happen in a separate sentence.

My cousin's baby gurgled in the middle of the carpeted living room, and mourners moved around her, tall legs gathering near a cheese plate.

This sentence is trying to adopt the baby's perspective—not a bad idea. But don't those tall legs sound disembodied? They may have gathered near a cheese plate, but one wonders how they managed to eat.

But when the Plains Indians hunted bison, they used every bit of the kill, from its meat to its dung and its hooves to its bone marrow; whites were notoriously wasteful.

Two sentences to begin with. Notice the awkwardness of the "from . . . to" structure, which implies a spectrum of possibilities. It's nearly always awkward. Instead: *they used every bit of the kill—meat, dung, hooves, bone marrow, and so on.*

And despite Crosby's distinguishable crooning, *White Christmas*'s Danny Kaye always got the laughs.

What does "distinguishable" mean here? It means that when Bing Crosby croons, we can tell he's crooning. The author probably means "distinctive." And note what this sentence doesn't say: Bing Crosby and Danny Kaye are both in *White Christmas*. This sentence makes it sound as though only Kaye is.

———————

She exasperatedly cleans it up with her napkin and gets him more milk.

It takes only a fleeting thought to realize that "exasperatedly" is grotesque, a destroyer of rhythm. The writer will need to convey exasperation some other way.

———————

I had to travel to Spain to see smoking on widespread display.

Note how inactive and unpeopled this is. Smoking is on widespread display in Spain, but who's doing the smoking?

———————

The white steeple sits on the side of a hill across from the Long Ridge Tavern.

And yet one wonders what happened to the church beneath it. Steeples don't sit, except perhaps on the churches below them. They rise.

While one can lament the decrease in imagination that the television show's imagery perpetuates or the loss of emphasis placed on people's distinct intonation, such criticisms discredit the television version by comparison to an incorrigible other, not by its own merit.

One has to be *taught* to write like this. And then one has to be taught *not* to write like this. Barely intelligible.

Melissa later told me that a random man offered her $800 to spank him.

Whatever you think of this man, he was certainly not random. He was the very man who was going to offer Melissa $800 to spank him. "Random" has an actual meaning, and this is not it.

The air was hot and damp under the awning of branches and leaves that hung over us.

A common mistake—making explicit what's already implicit. *The air was hot and damp under the awning of branches and leaves.*

The 61–59 contest will be remembered by Duke's imposing size, Butler's resiliency, and the game's final play.

This sentence says that Duke's size, Butler's resilience, and the game's final play will remember the 61–59 contest. The problem? "By" instead of "for."

———————

In the last ten years or so, the revival of the Los Angeles River has emerged as a major policy priority, as activists have successfully convinced public officials that revitalizing the LA River will help them fix the city's worst troubles.

What is the word "as" doing here? Merely joining two sentences and making a single awkward one. Remove "as" and you have two passable sentences.

———————

Cacti are supposed to be the pinnacle of survival.

There's a thought here, though what it is is nearly impossible to say. "The pinnacle of survival" makes no sense. And note that "are supposed to be" could imply the author's disappointment with cacti.

———————

My mom and I drove to where the flames were.
Or perhaps *drove toward the fire?*

Acknowledgments

Thanks to Dan Frank and, as always, to Flip Brophy. I'm grateful for support from the Ucross Foundation and the John Simon Guggenheim Memorial Foundation. I've been aided and helpfully challenged by colleagues in several English departments, including those at Fordham University, where I first started teaching creative writing, Harvard University, and, especially, Pomona College.

My greatest debt is to my students over the past thirty years. They've taught me far more than I've ever managed to teach them, and they've made teaching writing one of the great joys of my life.

"Charming and most enjoyable."
—*The New York Times*

TIMOTHY, OR NOTES OF AN ABJECT REPTILE

Few writers have attempted to explore the natural history of a particular animal by adopting the animal's own sensibility. But Verlyn Klinkenborg has done just that in *Timothy*: an insightful and utterly engaging story of the world's most famous tortoise, whose real life was observed by the eighteenth-century English curate and naturalist Gilbert White. For thirteen years, Timothy lived in White's garden. Here Klinkenborg gives the tortoise an unforgettable voice and keen powers of observation on both human and natural affairs. Wry and wise, unexpectedly moving and enchanting at every careful turn, *Timothy* surprises and delights.

Fiction/Nature

VINTAGE BOOKS
Available wherever books are sold.
www.vintagebooks.com